Tickle Your Pickle with Shedletskys

How to make (& eat) handmade pickles, ferments & brines

James Cooper & Natalie Preston

Photography by
Mowie Kay

RYLAND PETERS & SMALL

Senior Editor Abi Waters
Senior Designer Toni Kay
Editorial Director Julia Charles
Creative Director Leslie Harrington
Production Manager Gordana Simakovic
Food Stylist Troy Willis
Props Stylist Max Robinson
Indexer Vanessa Bird

First published in 2025 by
Ryland Peters & Small
20–21 Jockey's Fields
London WC1R 4BW
and
1452 Davis Bugg Road,
Warrenton, NC 27589

www.rylandpeters.com
email: euregulations@rylandpeters.com

10 9 8 7 6 5 4 3 2 1

The authorised representative in the EEA is
Authorised Rep Compliance Ltd.,
Ground Floor, 71 Lower Baggot Street,
Dublin, D02 P593, Ireland
www.arccompliance.com

NOTES
• Both British (Metric) and American
(Imperial plus US cups) measurements
are included in these recipes for your
convenience; however it is important to
work with only one set of measurements
and not alternate between the two
within a recipe.
• All eggs are medium (UK) or large (US),
unless specified as large, in which case
US extra-large should be used. Uncooked
or partially cooked eggs should not
be served to the very old, frail, young
children, pregnant women or those
with compromised immune systems.
• See page 19 for notes on sterilizing
preserving jars.

DISCLAIMER
The views expressed in this book are those
of the author but they are general views
only and readers are urged to consult a
relevant and qualified specialist or
physician for individual advice on food
safety. Ryland Peters & Small hereby
exclude all liability to the extent permitted
by law for any errors or omissions in this
book and for any loss, damage or expense
(whether direct or indirect) suffered by a
third party relying on any information
contained in this book.

MIX
Paper | Supporting
responsible forestry
FSC® C008047

Contents

Introduction   6

Pickling Basics   8

Pickles in Practice   26

Cooking with Pickles   64

Some Sandwiches   96

A Bit on the Side   118

Index   142

Acknowledgements   144

Introduction

In 1923 my great-grandfather, Sam Shedletsky, opened a butcher's shop in East London. Our family has been helping people preserve food, in one way or another, ever since.

For four generations now, we've worked hard to ensure people always have good things to eat. The joy of feeding friends and family; the communal experience of good food shared with those you love; the simple but profound pleasures to be found in preserving, pickling, curing and fermenting – you could say, there's brine in our blood.

My gran, Freda, grew up living above Sam's butcher's shops in Stepney Green and, later, Brixton Market. She married Harry Cooper in the 1940s and the newly-weds soon left the butchery business behind. They didn't stray too far from food though; in the early 1950s they opened a small shop selling domestic fridges and freezers so people could better preserve food at home.

Jump forward a few decades, and my dad took over the family business. He probably would have been perfectly happy selling fridges, cookers and dishwashers to the people of London, until my mum found herself the winner of an amateur cooking competition – a competition which, only a couple of years later, would change its name to MasterChef, and end up becoming part of the cultural landscape of cookery in the UK. Off the back of mum's culinary success, my parents upped sticks from London and opened a hotel-restaurant in a draughty manor house in the West Country. Which is where I come in.

Some of my earliest and most vivid memories are of the food my mum cooked in our hotel's kitchen. Slices of lemon tart, eaten under the big prep table. Jars of sun-dried tomatoes (it was the early 90s after all) stacked and waiting to be drained for the Provençal tart that guests couldn't get enough of. Getting involved in helping to make pasta and pastry, I found myself growing up around that chaotic but intoxicating buzz you only really get in a professional kitchen, as the act of feeding people becomes something more than just the fulfilment of a basic need.

It didn't work out in the end. Turns out, running a rural hotel and restaurant in the middle of a recession isn't a path to financial security when you've got two young kids and negative equity. Still, I was left with a deep love of food and of feeding people, a passion that would endure through a few less-than-ideal early jobs in journalism and advertising. As much as I loved food and cooking, however, it wasn't really something I could see myself doing professionally – where would I even begin?

That all changed when I met Nat – as it happens, at a music festival just a stone's throw from Sam's original butcher's shop in East London. Luckily, Nat also loved feeding people. Early in our relationship we'd regularly host dinner parties at our tiny Dalston flat, making increasingly elaborate meals from our ever-growing collection of cookbooks. It was at one of these dinner parties – a Korean Easter celebration inspired by David Chang's brilliant *Momofuku* cookbook – that we first made kimchi. From that moment on, we were hooked on pickling and preserving.

We loved the fact that a few simple techniques and a bit of patience could produce food that was not only delicious, but stayed good for months. We soon started hosting Pickling Pop-Ups, inviting friends (and later strangers) into our flat to make kimchi or pickles with whatever vegetables looked good or were in season. A move to Leyton, and a remarkably run-down house, put paid to the pop-ups, but it turned out that people still wanted our pickles.

So late in 2019 we took the plunge and launched Shedletskys – named in honour of Sam and his butcher's shop – with a simple goal: to make and sell beautifully preserved pickles and ferments that use some of the world's oldest techniques, updated for the modern world.

In this book, you'll find a collection of recipes that showcase what we've learned about pickling since launching Shedletskys. They'll give you all the tools you need to get started with pickling, as well as recipes and ideas for what you can do with your pickles once they are ready to eat.

We hope you'll have as much fun making, sharing and eating them as we have had on our own pickling journey.

Pickling Basics

PICKLING AT ITS MOST BASIC

For us, this is where it all began. Years before we were filling 180-litre/40-gallon barrels with pungent fermenting cabbage or plunging industrial quantities of cucumbers into bubbling vats of vinegar, we were making instant pickles at home to bring a bit of zip, zing and freshness to our dinners and sandwiches.

This is pickling at its most basic. There's no vinegar, so unlike their traditionally brined or fermented cousins, these pickles don't require weeks or months of patience before they can be consumed. Instead, they deliver a burst of flavour in as little as 30 minutes, making them perfect when you need to add a little sumthin' sumthin' to a weeknight dinner, supercharge a bland salad or just find yourself dangerously short of pickles.

Despite the speed and simplicity, this pickling technique is also your secret weapon against lacklustre supermarket produce. A quick pickle can brighten up a watery cucumber or a less-than-perfect tomato like nothing else. And the beauty of this method really does lie in its simplicity. There's no need to sterilize anything and you don't need any specialized equipment. All you need is a bowl, some vegetables, salt, sugar and a little patience.

The big downside is that these pickles won't last as long as traditional pickles. You'll need to eat them within a few hours or risk finding that your vegetables have turned to mush.

The Shedletskys' quick pickle method: no vinegar needed

Lots of quick pickle recipes call for vinegar. But our approach is even simpler. We rely on the power of salt and sugar to draw out moisture from the vegetables, creating a simple brine that's both flavourful and leaves the vegetables crunchy and delicious in a matter of minutes.

VEGETABLES TO TRY:

Tomatoes

Cucumbers

Radishes

Celery

Carrots

Shallots

Beetroot/beets (thinly sliced)

Celeriac/celery root (thinly sliced)

VEGETABLES TO AVOID:

Onions (they need a longer pickling time to mellow their flavour)

Delicate greens (such as lettuce, which will go mushy)

Vegetables that can't be eaten raw (like potatoes)

Ingredients for Instant Pickled Tomato and Cucumber Salad (see page 53).

1 Weigh the vegetables

The key to success with these quick pickles is accurate measurements. Start by weighing the vegetables you plan to pickle. This will be your base number for calculating the quantities of salt and sugar. Obviously, a set of kitchen scales is your best friend here.

2 Calculate the salt

In all cases and whatever vegetables you're using, you'll need 2.5% of the weight of your vegetables in salt. Lots of people freak out when confronted with the calculation, but it's pretty simple.

Let's say you have 200 g/7 oz. sliced cucumbers. Simply divide 200 (the weight of your vegetables) by 100 and multiple the resulting number by 2.5. In this case, $200 \div 100 = 2$. And 2×2.5 is 5. So you would need to add 5 g/$\frac{1}{5}$ oz. salt to the prepared vegetables.

An even easier way to do this is to multiply the weight of the vegetables in grams/ounces by 0.025 to get the correct amount of salt in grams/ounces.

3 Calculate the sugar

Next, calculate the weight of sugar needed. This is a bit more dependent on the vegetables you're using and your own personal preferences, but a good place to start is with 5% of the weight of your vegetables in sugar. You could calculate this in exactly the same way as above. Or just double the salt quantity for a quick and easy calculation.

4 Prepare, combine and toss

Place the prepared vegetables in a bowl (see opposite for some preparation tips). Add the calculated amount of salt and toss to coat evenly. Add the sugar and toss again.

5 Rest then taste

Let the vegetables sit at room temperature, covered, for at least 30 minutes. During this time, the salt and sugar will draw out moisture, creating a flavourful brine.

After 30 minutes, taste a piece. If it needs a bit more sweetness to balance the saltiness, add a little more sugar, a pinch at a time, until it reaches your desired flavour.

ADDING FLAVOUR

While the salt and sugar create a delicious base, you can elevate your quick pickles with herbs and spices. Add about 1 teaspoon of your chosen flavourings per 200 g/7 oz. of chopped vegetables. Pop the herbs and spices in when you add the salt and sugar at Step 4 (prepare, combine and toss).

Have fun and play around. But to get started, here are some combinations we've had success with:

Tomatoes: *Dried oregano and fresh basil*

Cucumbers: *Dried chilli flakes/hot red pepper flakes and ground coriander seeds*

Radishes: *Chinese five-spice and Sichuan peppercorns*

Celery: *Fresh dill and mustard seeds*

VEGETABLE PREPARATION TIPS

These pickles are super forgiving, but there are a few things you can do to make sure they turn out as tasty as possible.

Slice evenly: *Aim for regular, bite-sized pieces. This ensures that the salt and sugar penetrate evenly and that the pickles are easy to eat.*

Remove seeds: *For cucumbers and tomatoes, we recommend removing the seeds. Cut them in half and scoop out the seeds with a teaspoon. This prevents the pickles from becoming too watery.*

Wash, don't peel: *There's no need to peel most vegetables for quick pickling. Just give them a good wash and allow them to drain before adding the salt, sugar and flavourings.*

Slice finely: *For particularly dense vegetables such as beetroot/beet and celeriac/celery root, it's best to slice them very finely to achieve a good crunch and pickled finish.*

STORING QUICK PICKLES

These pickles are best enjoyed fresh. In fact, they'll start to soften after a few hours and will be alarmingly soft and mushy not long after that. If you need to prepare them in advance, it is best to opt for harder vegetables – such as carrots and radishes – and store them, covered, in the fridge for no more than 6 hours.

If you're looking to actively preserve your vegetables over a longer time frame, this is not the technique for you! I'd recommend heading to the next section to explore some more long-lasting pickling techniques, if that is the case.

VINEGAR-BRINED PICKLES

While our quick fridge pickles offer instant gratification and are useful when speed is paramount, it's the vinegar-brined beauties that most people think of when they hear the word pickle. Ultimately, we're talking about vegetables submerged in a tangy, flavourful vinegar-based brine that kills off bad bacteria and keeps the vegetables preserved. But the devil's in the detail here and there are two techniques that we use to pickle things in vinegar. Hot brining involves heating a vinegar mixture with flavourings to boiling point to dissolve everything before pouring over your prepared vegetables. Cold brining is even simpler: just prep your vegetables and spices and pour vinegar over them. Which you choose depends on the vegetables involved and the desired pickle style.

Hot vs. cold – choosing your technique

It will come as a surprise to no one that the main difference between hot and cold vinegar brining lies in the temperature of the brine when it's added to the vegetables.

There are lots of competing claims about the benefits of the two techniques, as well as whether one method or the other is better for preservation. But in our experience, most of the difference comes down to what the heat of the vinegar does to the texture of the vegetables.

In almost all cases, the salt and acid of the vinegar is what's doing the preservation rather than any heat. So have a go at both and decide for yourself which one delivers the sort of results you personally enjoy.

For all of the recipes for vinegar-brined pickles in this book, you can happily swap techniques. Just be aware the final texture might be impacted.

HOT BRINING

Here the vinegar, water, salt, sugar and any spices are heated together to create a hot brine into which the vegetables are submerged. This slight cooking of the vegetables leads to a softer texture, making it ideal for tougher vegetables like carrots and thick-skinned cucumbers and when you want to take the harsh edge off garlic and onions. The heat also allows for deeper penetration of flavours, especially from spices. Hot brining can also create a partial vacuum when the jars are sealed, contributing to a longer shelf life.

It's also our preferred method when using less acidic brines like rice wine vinegar, as the heat helps to further inhibit bacterial growth.

COLD BRINING

As the name suggests, this method uses a room-temperature brine. The vegetables remain essentially raw, resulting in a crisp, crunchy texture.

The issue here is that it is far easier to dissolve the salt, sugar and spices in a heated liquid so we often heat the brine to mix, then leave it to cool before adding the vegetables. If you're impatient, consider dissolving things in half the specified quantity of vinegar and then adding the rest to help cool the liquid.

Cold brining is perfect for delicate vegetables like radishes, celery, turnips and daikon, as well as some fruits, where maintaining that fresh, crisp bite is essential.

While flavour development may take a bit longer, the vibrant texture is often worth the wait.

COLD BRINING DELICATE FRUITS AND VEGETABLES

Cold brining is generally used for more delicate vegetables such as radishes, celery and some fruits. This means that the fresh crispness of the vegetables or fruit will be maintained.

A NOTE ON VINEGAR

Unlike our quick fridge pickles, which rely solely on salt and sugar, vinegar is doing much of the heavy lifting here. As such the vinegar you choose is important. For all vinegar-brined pickles, we recommend sticking to neutral-flavoured vinegars with at least 5% acidity. This ensures proper preservation and allows the flavours of the vegetables and spices to shine through. In our factory, we use distilled white vinegar. A lot of white vinegar. Generally enough to make the delivery drivers hate us.

Distilled white vinegar is cost-effective, readily available and has a clean, neutral taste. White wine vinegar is another excellent option as an alternative.

Keep your fancier vinegars (like balsamic or sherry vinegar) for salad dressings or other applications where their distinct flavours will be appreciated.

The one exception is rice wine vinegar, which we often use when creating pickles with an Asian-inspired flavour profile. Its mild sweetness and delicate aroma complement many Asian vegetables and spices beautifully. Just be aware rice wine vinegar is a bit less acidic so these pickles will probably not last as long as those made with stronger distilled white vinegar.

Finally, it's probably worth avoiding strongly flavoured, dark vinegars like malt vinegar unless you specifically want that particular flavour in your pickles.

A WORD ON RATIOS

The specific ratio of vinegar to water in your brine will depend on the recipe and your desired level of tartness. As a general guideline, we typically use either straight vinegar or somewhere near 2:1 ratio of vinegar to water.

Straight vinegar: *This creates the most intensely flavoured and longest-lasting pickles.*

2:1 vinegar to water: *This offers a milder flavour while still providing excellent preservation. Make sure the vegetables are properly salted to ensure they stay fresh.*

You can experiment with ratios up to 1:1 vinegar to water, but be aware that pickles made with lower vinegar concentrations have a shorter shelf life and should always be stored in the fridge. In semi-fermented pickles like our Curtido (see page 57) we alter the brine's pH through the activity of good bacteria that makes fermentation happen. Check out the next chapter for a more detailed explanation.

A CRUCIAL POINT

No matter the ratio, the most crucial factor is ensuring the vegetables are completely submerged in the brine. This prevents spoilage and ensures even pickling. The easiest way to do this is with a set of glass fermentation weights that can be added just before the jars are sealed to make sure nothing pokes out of the brine and spoils.

If you don't have weights (or as often happens at home with us, all of them are already in play in other pickle jars), you can create an alternative with a sealable plastic sandwich bag. Simply make sure the one you use is the right size – small enough to fit inside the jar, but large enough to cover the pickles – and half fill with cold water. Make sure the bag is completely sealed and then use to weigh down the pickles as you would with a weight.

If you're really getting into pickling, we recommend investing in a digital food pH tester. They can be bought relatively cheaply online and can be used to measure the acidity of the brine before you seal the jars. We check the pH of every batch of pickles we make to ensure it's at a safe level, but at home you probably only need one if you're going to be making a lot of experimental pickles!

SOMETHING SWEET

While vinegar and salt are the primary preservatives, creating an environment where harmful bacteria struggles to survive, sugar plays an important role in balancing the flavour of vinegar-brined pickles. Without it, your pickles will be one-dimensional and probably aggressively sour.

One thing to note – often we make brines that are a little sweeter than you might expect when you first make your pickles. This is because the vegetables will sometimes continue to either ferment (slowly) in their brine or extrude additional water, diluting the flavour over time. To counteract this, we sweeten the brines at the start.

LEAVING SPACE FOR THINGS TO BREATHE

When it comes to filling the jars, remember to leave a couple of centimetres/an inch of space between the top of the pickles/brine and the rim of the jar. This allows for a little bit of expansion, which is crucial if any slight fermentation occurs. While vinegar-brined pickles are generally less active than lacto-fermented pickles, it's always a good idea to leave a little breathing room.

Cold brining

Cold brining pickles is pretty simple. To ensure a good flavour penetration and to slightly speed up the process, some recipes suggest salting the prepared vegetables ahead of time. Then follow this step-by-step process:

1 Prepare the brine

In a bowl, combine the vinegar, water, salt, sugar and any desired spices according to the recipe. Stir until the salt and sugar are completely dissolved. You may need to gently warm the mixture to help with dissolving, but do not boil.

2 Fill the jars

Pack the prepared vegetables into sterilized jars (see opposite).

3 Pour the brine

Make sure the brine is completely cold, then pour it over the vegetables, leaving a couple of centimetres/ an inch of headspace.

4 Seal the jars

Use a weight to ensure the pickles remain submerged at all times. Place the sterilized lids on the jars and tighten the rings.

STORAGE

All our vinegar-brined pickles, whether hot or cold processed, must be stored in the fridge. They will typically last for a couple of months, and potentially even longer.

HOT BRINING GREEN TOMATOES
As the name suggests, this method uses a heated brine, which leads to a softer texture, making it ideal for thicker-skinned vegetables.

Hot brining

1 Prepare the brine

In a large, non-reactive saucepan (stainless steel or enamel), combine the vinegar, water, salt, sugar and any desired spices according to the recipe.

2 Heat and dissolve

Heat the mixture over a medium heat, stirring continuously, until the salt and sugar are completely dissolved. Bring to the boil.

3 Let the vinegar get to know the vegetables

You can do this in one of two ways:

Cook the vegetables briefly in the brine – *for some recipes, you add the prepared vegetables directly to the boiling brine and cook them for a specified time (as in our Bread and Butter Pickles on page 58).*

Decant immediately and let the residual heat do the job – *in most cases, you drop the vegetables into the liquid, immediately remove the pan from the heat and proceed to the next step. You can also skip the submersion and simply pour the hot brine over the vegetables in the sterilized jar.*

4 Fill the jars

Remove the prepared vegetables from the hot brine and place them into the sterilized jars first. Carefully pour the hot brine over them, leaving a couple of centimetres/ an inch of headspace. This also gently heats the glass, reducing the risk of it cracking from thermal shock.

5 Seal the jars

Immediately place the sterilized lids on the jars and tighten the rings, then check the seal following the instructions below.

CHECKING THE SEAL ON HOT-BRINED PICKLES

We prefer to cool our hot-brined pickles upside down. Simply invert the jars after sealing and place on a tray to cool. This allows us to quickly see if any jars haven't sealed properly (they'll leak!) and creates a vacuum seal as the contents cool. Once the jars are cool, turn them the right way up and store in the fridge.

If you're using jars with less reliable seals, instead of inverting them, use a weight (like a fermentation weight) to keep the pickles submerged in the brine. As long as the jars were properly sterilized and the vegetables are submerged, a perfect seal is less critical for preservation.

LET'S TALK ABOUT STERILIZATION

OK. Listen up. This bit is boring but critical for safe pickling.

Before you begin making vinegar-brined pickles (or any fermented beauties, but we'll get to that in a few pages), it's crucial to sterilize the jars and lids properly. This process eliminates most bacteria or microorganisms that could spoil the pickles. It's also why we recommend using proper glass jars with lids for pickling as these are relatively easy to sterilize.

It should go without saying, but… work clean. That means wash your hands thoroughly with soap and water before you start pickling. Clean all surfaces and utensils that will come into contact with the pickles properly, and make sure your produce is washed thoroughly.

HOW TO STERILIZE JARS AND LIDS

1 Wash jars, bottles and lids in warm, soapy water, then rinse thoroughly.

2 Apply some heat by either:

Putting them in the oven for 20 minutes – *place jars and lids on a baking sheet and heat in a preheated oven at 140°C/120°C fan/ 285°F/Gas 1 for 20 minutes.*

Dropping them into boiling water – *place jars and lids in a large saucepan and cover completely with water. Ensure there are no air bubbles trapped inside. Bring the water to the boil and boil for at least 10 minutes.*

3 Remove the sterilized jars and lids from the oven or boiling water using heatproof tongs. Fill them immediately with the prepared pickles and brine.

FERMENTED PICKLES

Some of Shedletskys most popular products – our kimchi, curtido and several of our hot sauces – all rely on the power of fermentation for their flavour and as a means of keeping them from spoiling.

As a technique, lacto-fermentation uses the power of beneficial bacteria to transform vegetables into something truly special. Unlike vinegar brining, which relies on added acidity, lacto-fermentation creates its own acidity through the natural action of *Lactobacillus* bacteria. This process not only preserves the vegetables but also develops complex flavours and results in foods that are great for your gut health.

Understanding the process

In essence, when we ferment food, we're simply trying to promote the growth of 'good' bacteria, primarily Lactobacillus, *while suppressing 'bad' bacteria, like* Clostridium botulinum, *that can cause food to spoil.*

The secret weapon in this battle is salt; by creating a particularly salty environment that the vegetables sit in, you in turn stop the growth of harmful bacteria while allowing Lactobacillus *to thrive.*

Opposite: Dry salting Chinese leaf cabbage.

'Don't Call it Kimchi' Lacto-fermented Chinese Leaf Cabbage (see page 54) and Lacto-pickled Pineapple Salsa (see page 42).

This process happens over two main stages:

1 **Suppression:** *Initially, salt creates an environment where harmful bacteria struggle to survive. This gives the naturally present* Lactobacillus *bacteria a competitive advantage.*

2 **Lactic acid production:** *Over time, the* Lactobacillus *bacteria start consuming the sugars present in the vegetables. As they do, they produce lactic acid as a byproduct. This lactic acid gradually lowers the pH of the brine, creating an acidic environment that further inhibits the growth of undesirable microorganisms. This acidity is what gives lacto-fermented foods their characteristic tangy flavour.*

In many of the recipes in this book, we add some vinegar into the mix, which helps preserve the food more quickly as we're not waiting for the Lactobacillus *bacteria to produce lactic acid to drop the pH to safe levels. The trade off is that fermentation is considerably slower and so full flavours can take longer to develop.*

FEELING A BIT SALTY

Salt is absolutely essential for successful lacto-fermentation. It plays multiple crucial roles:

Creating the right environment
Salt promotes the growth of beneficial *Lactobacillus* while suppressing harmful bacteria.

Preserving texture
Salt helps to keep vegetables crisp by slowing down the processes that makes them go soft.

Enhancing flavour
Obviously salt is delicious so adding a bit to vegetables is never a bad thing and helps bring out the other flavours of the pickles and ferments.

Extracting water
When we dry salt vegetables, it draws out moisture, improving the texture.

The most important thing to remember when it comes to the salt for pickling and fermenting is to use non-iodized salt that doesn't have any anti-caking agents in it. Any sea salt will do. Just remember to check the ingredients on the packaging of the salt before you start as added chemicals can inhibit fermentation and affect the flavour of the final pickle.

FINDING BALANCE

Getting the salt concentration right is vital when pickling and fermenting. Too little and you don't create a hostile environment for the bad bacteria. Too much and you risk making the environment too hostile for even the *Lactobacillus* bacteria to thrive (plus it'll taste pretty unpleasant!). In general, a ratio of between 3–5% salt is a good place to start.

There are two main approaches to salting vegetables in this book.

Dry salting: *This method is used for vegetables with a high water content, like cabbage (think kimchi or sauerkraut). The vegetables are chopped or shredded, then sprinkled with salt. The salt draws out the vegetables' natural juices, creating a brine. Vigorous mixing, massaging or even 'bashing' the vegetables helps to release more liquid.*

Brining: *For vegetables with a lower water content, a separate salt brine is prepared. The vegetables are submerged in this brine, ensuring they are completely covered. In these instances, calculate the salt percentage against the brine liquid, rather than the vegetables.*

FERMENTATION WEIGHTS

Glass weights are useful for ensuring the vegetables stay well submerged in the brine, making a more successful pickle.

FORMING OF FERMENTATION BUBBLES

Generally this is a good visible sign that Lactobacillus *is active and that lacto-fermentation is happening. You can find out about other signs below.*

A NICE BIT OF KIT

You don't need a lot of fancy equipment for lacto-fermentation, but a few key items are helpful.

Vessels: *Glass jars or ceramic crocks are the best choices. While some people use plastic containers, we prefer to avoid them at home.*

Weights: *Keeping the vegetables completely submerged in the brine is absolutely critical for successful lacto-fermentation. This creates an anaerobic environment (without oxygen) that promotes the growth of beneficial bacteria and prevents mould. You can use specialized fermentation weights (often made of glass), or you can improvise with a small, clean, sealable plastic sandwich bag filled with water or brine.*

Airlocks (optional): *Fermentation airlocks are lids with a valve that allow carbon dioxide (a byproduct of fermentation) to escape while preventing oxygen from entering. They're helpful but not strictly necessary. If you don't use an airlock, you'll need to 'burp' your jars daily by briefly opening them to release any built-up gas.*

pH metre (optional): *Available to buy online, these quickly show you the acidity of your ferments so you can see the pH dropping as the* Lactobacillus *does its job.*

SIGNS OF SUCCESS

Once you've salted the vegetables and got them into the brine, the two main factors that come into play are time and temperature. The ideal temperature range for lacto-fermentation is 15–24°C/59–75°F, which is essentially room temperature, so that part is easy. Just leave the ferments on the side in the kitchen and keep an eye on them. Placing jars on a tray is a good idea just in case things get over vigorous or particularly bubbly!

Over a couple of days, as the vegetables ferment, you'll see signs that the process is working, such as:

Bubbles: *The formation of bubbles is a good indication that* Lactobacillus *is active and producing carbon dioxide.*

Cloudy brine: *Some cloudiness is normal as flavours develop.*

However, there are also signs that something might be going wrong:

Excessively cloudy brine: *While some cloudiness is normal, an extremely cloudy brine can be a sign things have gone wrong along the way.*

Dark mould: *If you see black mould, or if white mould reappears after you've scraped it off, discard the ferment.*

Flavours usually develop nicely after about a week of fermentation at room temperature, but the exact time will vary depending on the temperature, the type of vegetable and your personal preference.

TASTE TEST

The best way to determine if your ferment is ready is to taste it! Start tasting after a few days and continue until it reaches the desired level of sourness and tanginess. Now you can slow down the process significantly by transferring it to the fridge. The cold temperature slows down the activity of the *Lactobacillus*. In some cases, particularly with vigorous ferments, the pH will eventually drop low enough to naturally kill off the bacteria, effectively stopping fermentation. We also add vinegar to some pickles to achieve the same effect. Many of the recipes in this book incorporate vinegar, creating a hybrid between a pickle and a true ferment. The addition of vinegar further lowers the pH, contributing to both flavour and preservation.

MULTI-USE FERMENTS

These lacto-fermented pickles can be enjoyed in so many ways. Here, our take on kimchi (see page 54) has been chopped and added to a quick dish of fried rice and vegetables.

Pickles
in Practice

Classic deli dill-pickled cucumber

This is it. The bubbe *pickle of Jewish deli culture. It's the pickle that most people probably think of when you tell them you make pickles for a living. But here's the thing. For the longest time, we steered clear of making them, especially commercially for Shedletskys. Why? Well, as a pickle that entirely relies on salt to preserve them, they are a little tricky to get right. Relying on a salt brine means that however carefully you sterilize things and keep your surfaces clean, sometimes things go wrong. In a commercial setting, this is a problem. You can get consistency by adding preservatives, but we didn't want to do that in any of our products. So these incredible pickles remain an at-home treat for us.*

Accuracy is critical if you want to give yourself the best chance of success with these pickles. That's why we always suggest weighing the salt and water used here rather than relying on spoon measurements.

8 small Persian cucumbers
  (about 1 kg/2¼ lb.)

50 g/3½ tablespoons salt

3 garlic cloves, peeled and lightly
  crushed/minced

1 tablespoon black peppercorns

1 tablespoon yellow mustard seeds

1 teaspoon dill seeds (optional)

3 dried bay leaves

2-cm/¾-inch strip of kombu
  (optional)

10 g/⅓ oz. fresh dill fronds

*a large 2-litre/quart preserving jar
  (or something that will comfortably
  accommodate the cucumbers with
  about 3 cm/1¼ inches headroom)*

*fermentation weight (or water-filled,
  sealable plastic sandwich bag)*

Makes 1 large jar

Slice the bottoms and tops off the cucumbers and place in a large bowl. Fill with very cold water and add a few ice cubes to keep the cucumbers really cold while you prepare the brine. (Keeping the vegetables chilled helps to preserve their crunch later in the pickling process.)

In a separate bowl, measure exactly 1 litre/4 cups (or 1 kg/2¼ lb. if using a digital scale) water from the tap. Add the salt and whisk vigorously until the salt is completely dissolved. Add the garlic, peppercorns, mustard seeds and dill seeds (if using) to the brine. Stir to distribute everything in the brine.

Remove the cucumbers from their ice bath. Arrange in a large sterilized jar so they are standing on their ends. Add the bay leaves, kombu (if using) and dill fronds and carefully pour in the brine to cover. Make sure all of the spices go into the jar along with the brine.

Weigh down the cucumbers so they are completely submerged using a fermentation weight or a water-filled, sealable plastic sandwich bag. Leave on the side until bubbles start to form – usually after a couple of days. At this point start testing the pickles. There should be a pleasant, slightly sour taste. This will develop further the longer you leave them. We like our pickles after about a week of fermentation, but feel free to experiment to your own taste.

Once you are happy with how the pickles taste, pop them in the fridge to slow down the fermentation. They will continue to ferment, getting softer and more sour and will still be tasty up to 6 weeks after you made them. (We have had batches that are still delicious 3 months after we made them.)

If at any point the pickles go mouldy or the brine becomes excessively cloudy, discard them and chalk the failed batch down to experience.

Cajun pickled peppers

Early in the Shedletskys journey, we started buying our vegetables from New Spitalfields Market in East London. It's an incredible place: a vast 31-acre site that's home to more than 100 traders who sell literally every sort of vegetable imaginable. Great if you ever need to start ordering cucumbers in significant numbers and are happy arguing over the price of tomatoes at 5am, but navigating its opaque buying processes takes some getting used to.

This recipe is the result of an early SNAFU. I had thought I was buying several boxes of the green cayenne chillies for our hot sauce. Instead, what arrived was actually a selection of much milder Turkish peppers. Not keen to see them go to waste, we worked up a recipe for a pickle that works just as well as an accompaniment to a falafel wrap as it does as part of the Holy Trinity, so vital to much of the cooking of Louisiana and the Deep South.

10 long mild Turkish peppers
   (see Note), about 500 g/
   18 oz. in weight
4 garlic cloves
300 ml/1¼ cups white vinegar
20 g/¾ oz. white sugar
40 g/1½ oz. salt
1 teaspoon celery seeds
1 teaspoon cumin seeds
1 teaspoon black peppercorns
1 teaspoon yellow mustard seeds
2 bay leaves

Makes 1 large jar

Give the peppers a thorough wash in cold water and leave to drain. Prick each pepper a couple of times with the point of a sharp knife to allow the brine to penetrate more easily. Arrange in a large sterilized jar so they are standing on their ends. Peel the garlic and crush each clove with the back of a knife, then add to the jar with the peppers.

Make a brine in a saucepan by mixing 700 ml/3 cups water with the white vinegar and heating gently. Add the sugar and salt, then stir to dissolve.

Measure out all of the spices and add to the jar along with the peppers and garlic. Add the bay leaves, seal the jar and shake well to make sure all of the spices are well distributed.

When the brine comes to the boil and the sugar and salt are dissolved, open the jar and carefully pour the brine over the contents. Push down the peppers so they are covered by the brine and secure using a fermentation weight. Leave to cool before sealing the jar and storing in the fridge.

The pickles will be ready to eat after 48 hours, but will get even better over the next week or so, and last more than 6 weeks when stored in the fridge.

A NOTE ON THE PEPPERS

We use a mixture of different varieties of Turkish peppers here, including the Sivri and Charlston varieties. They were what our local Turkish supermarket had in stock, but you can use any mild green peppers here. Or mix in a few hotter ones and play 'pepper roulette'!

'Pukka' pickled watermelon rinds

I was 16 when The Naked Chef *first aired on TV, which means I was 16 when I first heard the idea of cutting a hole in a watermelon and filling it with vodka. For the entire summer after GCSEs, my friends and I were obsessed. We took illicitly boozy watermelons to Glastonbury (where they were devoured watching Moloko and James, if memory serves correctly) and to Newquay (where we thought giving out slices in the queue for Tall Trees nightclub would guarantee us entry – it didn't). Watermelons packed with the cheapest vodka came with us to house parties across the west country. They were everywhere. Until someone pointed out that it was much easier just to drink the vodka and not bother with the four days of gentle infusing that this 'cocktail' required.*

So I filed away Jamie's vodka watermelon somewhere in the back of my brain, until we were working up this recipe for pickled watermelon rinds. I was suddenly reminded of that sweet, warm, boozy tang from the summer of 1999 and thought a good hit of alcohol might elevate these pickles. Because we'd taken the pickling brine in a Mexican direction with lime and chipotle chilli, we swapped vodka for mescal but otherwise the idea remains, something I'm sure the Naked Chef would think was 'absolutely pukka'.

rind from 1 watermelon
(about 1 kg/2¼ lb.)

225 ml/1 cup minus 2 teaspoons
white vinegar

125 ml/½ cup rice vinegar

250 ml/1 cup watermelon juice
(flesh blitzed and strained)

½ tablespoon chipotle chilli flakes

juice of 4 limes

125 g/⅔ cup minus 2 teaspoons
white sugar

2 teaspoons salt

120 ml/½ cup mescal or tequila
(optional)

Makes 1 large jar

First, prepare the watermelon rind. Using a vegetable peeler, remove all of the tough green skin from the watermelon. (If you fancy making your own vinegar from page 141, this is a good starter. If not, simply discard.)

Cut the watermelon into quarters, then remove the flesh itself from the middle so you are left with the rind and about 0.5 cm/¼ inch of pink flesh. Cut this into 2-cm/¾-inch chunks.

Take the flesh itself and blitz in the blender to a purée. Strain and reserve 250 ml/1 cup of the juice for the brine. (Any leftover juice can be used in cocktails, to make sorbet or as part of a watermelon vinegar on page 141.)

In a large non-reactive saucepan, heat the reserved watermelon juice with the white and rice vinegars. Add the chilli flakes, lime juice, sugar and salt, then stir to dissolve. Bring to the boil over a gentle heat, and when it boils, add the watermelon rind. Cook for 2 minutes until the rind softens slightly.

Immediately remove the rind from the brine and add to a large sterilized jar. Pour the hot brine over the rind, then add the mescal or tequila (if using). Seal the jar and set aside to cool.

The pickles will be ready in 24 hours and last a couple of weeks when stored in the fridge.

Sweet/sour sumac pickled onions

One of Nat's foundational food memories is her dad's pickled onions. (Another is liberating a 'particularly tasty looking and large Spanish onion' from her parent's kitchen and eating it in secret in her room over several days, but that's another story.)

This isn't her dad's recipe – which is an absolutely classic British interpretation of a pickled onion. Instead, we've given our onions a sweet and sour vibe and vaguely Middle Eastern spin through the use of some fruit molasses and a healthy hit of citrus-sharp sumac. The result is something that is as good pepping up a cheese sandwich as it is cutting through a filled pita.

500 g/1 lb. 2 oz. red onions (about 6 onions)

1 tablespoon salt

350 ml/1½ cups red wine vinegar

100 ml/⅓ cup plus 1 tablespoon balsamic vinegar

2 tablespoons sour cherry or pomegranate molasses

2 garlic cloves, sliced

100 g/½ cup brown sugar

1 tablespoon sumac

½ tablespoon black peppercorns

Makes 1 large jar

Peel and slice the red onions, retaining the bottom ends and outer skins of two of the onions (these help colour the brine and bring a pleasing vibrant pinkness to this pickle). Thinly slice the onions into half moons. Place these in a colander/strainer in the sink and toss with the salt. Leave to drain for about 10 minutes while you prepare the brine.

Place the red wine and balsamic vinegars, molasses, garlic, sugar, sumac and peppercorns into a saucepan and gently heat until the sugar has dissolved and the brine is just starting to simmer.

Turn off the heat, then add the drained onions. Allow them to soften in the residual heat of the brine, stirring occasionally.

Place the reserved onion ends and skins into a large sterilized jar, followed by the salted sliced onions from the brine. Pour in any additional brine, making sure the onions are completely submerged. Seal the jar and set aside to cool.

Because this pickle is partially cooked, it will be ready to eat in a couple of hours, but leaving it in the fridge for a couple of days makes it even tastier. Stored in the fridge, these pickles will be good to eat for at least a month and potentially longer.

Vaguely Italian vegetable giardiniera

We first ate something like this pickle on a road trip that started in Miami and took us through the Carolinas, Tennessee, Mississippi and down through Louisiana, ending in New Orleans. A particular highlight towards the end of the trip was the incredible sandwiches that we enjoyed, including the famous muffuletta at Central Grocery (a version of which is on page 107), as well as the Nashville Hot (see page 104).

Giardiniera, with its crunchy and sharp vegetables, is a perfect accompaniment to fatty deli meats and cheese. As a nod to our trip, our version takes its cue from the region's 'Holy Trinity' of vegetables, swapping out the onions for fennel in deference to the pickle's at best loose Italian roots.

1 fennel bulb (about 200 g/7 oz.)

4 carrots (about 200 g/7 oz.)

3 celery sticks/ribs (about 200 g/7 oz.)

2 large green (bell) peppers (about 200 g/7 oz.)

½ head of cauliflower (about 200 g/7 oz.)

200 g/7 oz. green olives, stoned/pitted and halved

5 garlic cloves, peeled and lightly crushed

3 green chillies/chiles, chopped but not deseeded

35 g/1¼ oz. salt

2 dried bay leaves

1 teaspoon coriander seeds

1 teaspoon black peppercorns

1 teaspoon yellow mustard seeds

½ teaspoon celery seeds

½ teaspoon Italian herb mix (either store-bought or see Note to make your own)

500 ml/2 cups white wine vinegar

Makes 1 large jar

Wash all the vegetables thoroughly and drain. Cut the fennel, carrot, celery and green peppers into bite-sized pieces. Break the cauliflower florets into similar sized pieces. Add all the prepared vegetables to a large bowl with the olives, garlic and green chillies.

Add the salt and toss to make sure all of the vegetables are well coated and a brine is beginning to form. Cover the bowl with a clean dish towel and leave the vegetables in their brine for 4 hours.

After 4 hours, tip the vegetables into a large colander/strainer in the sink and rinse. Allow them to drain briefly before returning them to the bowl. Add the bay leaves, coriander seeds, black peppercorns, mustard seeds, celery seeds and the Italian herb mix and toss so all the vegetables are coated and the spices are well distributed.

Mix the white wine vinegar with 500 ml/2 cups water in a separate bowl or jug/pitcher and stir to combine. Pack the vegetable mix into a large sterilized jar and carefully pour the brine over the contents. Ensure the pickles are submerged with a fermentation weight, seal and place in the fridge.

The pickle will be ready to eat after 24 hours, and even better after 48 hours, and last at least one month when stored in the fridge.

FOR THE ITALIAN HERB MIX

Mix together 1 tablespoon each of dried basil, dried thyme, dried rosemary and dried marjoram with 2 tablespoons dried oregano. Store in an airtight container for up to 3 months.

Pickled mustard seeds

The first cookbook I remember getting was Nigel Slater's Real Food *as a Christmas gift in about 1997. And the first thing I remember cooking from it was his creamy sausage pasta with mustard. Returning from the shops, laden down with plump Italian sausages, orecchiette pasta, a bunch of basil and a pokey jar of wholegrain mustard, I carefully followed the recipe and was overjoyed at the results. Since then, I must have cooked that dish hundreds of times and I have come to realize the genius lies in the judicial application of wholegrain mustard. The tiny pops of flavour make it, cutting through the fat and cream in a way that a smooth mustard just wouldn't.*

These pickled mustard seeds go one step further, giving you the tool to add a pop of flavour to everything from salads to sandwiches. They even work stirred into a dish of creamy sausage pasta.

200 ml/¾ cup plus 1 tablespoon white vinegar

80 g/½ cup minus 2 teaspoons dark brown sugar

1 teaspoon salt

1 teaspoon mustard powder

2 dried bay leaves

½ teaspoon ground turmeric

150 g/1 cup yellow mustard seeds

30 ml/2 tablespoons mustard liquor (optional)

Makes 1 medium jar

Place the white vinegar, brown sugar, salt, mustard powder, bay leaves, turmeric and 100 ml/⅓ cup plus 1 tablespoon water into a small saucepan. Gently warm over a low heat and stir to dissolve the sugar and salt.

Add the mustard seeds to a separate small saucepan. Cover with tap water and bring to a rolling boil over a high heat. Once the water boils, remove from the heat and drain the seeds through a fine sieve/strainer. Rinse the seeds with cold water and return to the pan. Repeat this whole process twice more to remove some of the bitterness from the mustard seeds.

After the mustard seeds have been boiled, rinsed and drained three times in total, add them to the saucepan with the warm brine.

Turn the heat up to medium and bring up to a gentle simmer, stirring occasionally. Cook for about 15 minutes until the mustard seeds are looking plump and the liquid has reduced a little.

Immediately pour both the brine and mustard seeds into a sterilized jar. Add the mustard liquor, if using, and seal with the lid. Allow to cool completely, then place in the fridge.

Leave for at least 5 days for the flavour to develop and the bitterness to mellow before using them to add a burst of pickle-y pop to salads or sandwiches.

Alternatively, allow the pickle to sit for 2 weeks and then use the seeds to make your own mustard (see page 130).

Tzimmes pickled carrots

Tzimmes is an Ashkenazi stew of carrots and dried fruits. But that isn't what my grandmother Freda thought it was. Thanks to a comprehension error from her 1950s edition of Florence Greenberg's Jewish Cookbook, *she spent her life convinced Tzimmes was a dish of peas and carrots (the recipe for which appeared directly above the Tzimmes recipe in Florence's seminal tome).*

It's a shame because there really is something magical about the combination of carrots when cooked down with lots of citrus and dried fruits. Earthy and sweet, it's moreish and great with fatty meats and winter stews.

To make amends for Freda's mistake, here we've tried to capture some of the deliciousness of the real Tzimmes combo in a pickle.

8 large carrots (about 500 g/1 lb. 2 oz.)
a thumb-sized piece of fresh ginger
100 g/³⁄₄ cup raisins
2 cinnamon sticks
600 ml/2¹⁄₂ cups white vinegar
15 g/1 tablespoon salt
120 g/¹⁄₂ cup honey
1 orange
1 lemon
1 teaspoon yellow mustard seeds
¹⁄₂ teaspoon cumin seeds
2 dried bay leaves
1 teaspoon ground black pepper
5 whole cloves

Makes 1 large jar

Peel the carrots, cut each one in half, then slice into 1-cm/¹⁄₂-inch half moons. Peel the ginger and slice into matchsticks. Add both to a bowl along with the raisins. Toss to combine, then place the mixture into a large sterilized jar, along with the cinnamon sticks

Make a brine by combining the white vinegar, salt and honey in a small saucepan. Using a vegetable peeler, take 3 strips of orange peel and 3 strips of lemon peel and add them to the saucepan.

Gently heat the brine and stir until the honey and salt have dissolved. Add the yellow mustard seeds, cumin seeds, bay leaves, black pepper and cloves. Continue to heat the brine until it is just about to boil. Carefully pour the hot brine over the carrots, ensuring that all the spices are submerged in the jar.

Seal with the lid and set aside to cool, then store in the fridge.

The pickles will be ready to eat after 24 hours and even better after 48 hours, and last at least one month when stored in the fridge.

Lacto-pickled pineapple salsa

The best taco we ever had was (unsurprisingly) in Mexico City. Almost everywhere we ate in the city was fantastic, but one place really stood out. It was a tiny hole-in-the-wall restaurant called Los Cocuyos down a side street. There were plastic tables on the street, long queues and a huge bubbling pot of oil that was home to all the meats that went into the tacos. You simply ordered and the staff pulled out hunks of super tender meat to chop and build the tacos.

Because all the meats were cooked together, there was a danger the tacos could become a bit samey. However, there were some lovely herby fresh salsas and sauces you could add to bring the tacos alive.

One was a funky, fruity yellow sauce that was simply incredible. We never worked out exactly what went into it, but this fermented pineapple salsa captures some of the heat, tang and freshness of it.

1 medium pineapple
 (about 500 g/1 lb. 2 oz.)
30 g/2 tablespoons salt
50 g/2 tablespoons white sugar
3 jalapeño chillies/chiles
6 spring onions/scallions
2 tablespoons fresh mint leaves

Makes 1 medium jar

Carefully peel the pineapple, then cut into quarters. Once quartered, remove the core and cut the remaining flesh into 1-cm/½-inch chunks. Add to a large bowl along with the salt and sugar. Toss to combine.

Halve and deseed the chillies, then slice thinly. Do the same with the spring onions and add both to the bowl with the pineapple. Toss to combine.

Finely chop the fresh mint, add to the pickle mixture, then toss everything together one more time in the bowl.

Pack the pickle mixture into a sterilized jar. Make sure all the salt is in the jar along with the fruit and any brine that has been extruded already. Using a wooden spoon, gently muddle everything down a bit until more brine is released.

Pour 500 ml/2 cups water (or more if needed) over the mixture, making sure everything is submerged. Stir well to make sure all the salt is dissolved.

Weigh down the pickle so it is completely submerged using a fermentation weight or a water-filled, sealable plastic sandwich bag. Leave to ferment out of the fridge for 3–4 days, or until you see bubbles forming in the brine.

Taste the pickle and assess the flavour. Is it getting nicely sour? If yes, pop it in the fridge to slow the fermentation. If you want it to develop more flavour, leave it to ferment for longer on the side.

The pineapple will soften as it ferments, but this is no bad thing. It will remain good for at least a couple of weeks and maybe longer depending on how much sugar was in the pineapple itself.

If left longer, it will break down completely into something much more like a very thin jam that will be deep and funky in flavour.

Dr. Brown's pickled celery

You don't really see Dr. Brown's Cel-Ray Soda much in the UK. They used to serve it at the sadly missed Monty's Deli in East London, but since it closed a few years ago, Nat has had to get her supply by ordering in bulk from an American candy importer.

To be fair, it's not hard to see why a celery-flavoured soft drink might be a bit of a hard sell to most people. But it's actually delicious. Sort of like a more interesting lemonade with a pleasant herbaceous flavour. The sweet/tart taste of the soda pairs really well with fatty, smoky meats, explaining why the soda remains a staple of New York's best delis.

The last time Nat bought herself 48 cans of the stuff from her wholesale hookup, I persuaded her to part with a single can to see if the sweet, flavourful liquid would make an interesting base for a pickle brine. We decided to lean into the soda's sweetness and use a similar technique to the one we use with our Bread and Butter Pickles (see page 58), swapping the cucumbers for more celery, and it came out really well.

1 x 330-ml/1⅓ cups can Dr. Brown's Cel-Ray Soda (see Note below)

330 ml/1⅓ cups white vinegar

1 teaspoon fennel seeds

1 teaspoon celery seeds

½ teaspoon ground turmeric

½ teaspoon black peppercorns

4 garlic cloves

600 g/1 lb. 5 oz. bunch of celery, cut into sticks/ribs

20 g/¾ oz. salt

Makes 1 large jar

First, open the can of Cel-Ray Soda and leave for 30 minutes or so to allow it to go a little flat. Pour the soda into a large saucepan with the vinegar and bring to the boil. While the brine is heating, add the fennel seeds, celery seeds, turmeric and peppercorns. Peel the garlic cloves and lightly crush with the flat part of a knife before also adding to the brine.

Peel the celery to remove any stringy bits and then slice into 2.5-cm/1-inch pieces. Add to a bowl, tip in the salt and toss vigorously. Set aside for 30 minutes to let the salt draw out some of the water from the celery.

After 30 minutes, remove the celery from the bowl and tip directly into the bubbling saucepan of brine. Cook for a couple of minutes before removing the celery with a slotted spoon and packing into a large sterilized jar. Pour the hot brine over the contents and allow to cool slightly. Weigh the celery down with a fermentation weight or water-filled, sealable plastic sandwich bag. Once completely cool, seal the jar and store in the fridge.

The pickle will be ready to eat in 24 hours and last for up to one month when stored in the fridge.

NOTE
If you can't get hold of Dr. Brown's Cel-Ray Soda, you can use Sprite or other clear sparkling lemonade as a suitable alternative.

Borscht-style pickled beetroot

According to family legend, Sam Shedletsky's ancestors walked to the UK from Odessa in Ukraine. Inevitably, we felt we had to include a recipe for the classic borscht soup (see page 76). If truth be told, the combination of earthy beetroot, sour herbs and sharp vinegar is too good to restrict to only a soup. So we've taken the flavour profile of borscht and made it into a pickle here too.

Making it involves roasting the beetroot before pickling, but the resulting pickle lasts for ages. It serves as the base for our Pickled Beetroot Borscht (see page 76), as well as featuring in our Chopped Liver Sandwich (see page 112), where it provides a lovely counterpoint to the iron-y tang of the paté.

3–4 large beetroot/beets (about 1 kg/2¼ lb.), peeled but left whole

6 fresh dill sprigs

400 ml/1¾ cups white vinegar

60 g/½ cup plus 2 teaspoons white sugar

15 g/½ oz. salt

1 teaspoon dill seeds

1 teaspoon caraway seeds

2 dried bay leaves

50 ml/¼ cup vodka (optional)

Makes 1 large jar

Preheat the oven to 180°C/160°C fan/350°F/Gas 4.

Individually wrap each beetroot in foil and bake in the oven until the point of a knife goes in easily. The cooking time will depend on the size of your beetroot. Start checking them after about 1 hour and be prepared to wait as much as 2 hours if your beetroot are particularly large.

Allow the beetroot to cool slightly. Unwrap the beetroot and cut each one in half, then cut the halves into 0.5-cm/¼-inch slices (gloves are useful here to prevent your hands being stained pink).

Take a sterilized jar large enough to accommodate the beetroot and begin to fill it with a layer of the slices. Add a couple of sprigs of fresh dill as you go and continue layering up until the jar is three-quarters full.

Put the white vinegar and 400 ml/1¾ cup water in a saucepan and heat gently. Add the sugar and salt, then stir to dissolve. Add the dill seeds, caraway seeds and bay leaves.

Once the brine comes to the boil and the sugar is dissolved, carefully pour over the beetroot until it's completely submerged. If desired, at this point you can add the vodka into the mix. Allow to cool slightly, seal the jar and store in the fridge.

The pickles will be ready to eat after 24 hours and keep for up to one month when stored in the fridge.

Pink pickled turnips

I don't know if it's a widely held view, but we think the best bit of a falafel wrap is always the pickles that accompany it. And the best pickle of all the selection is the pink turnip.

It isn't the easiest pickle to find in stores, so we came up with our own version that captures the bright, spicy appeal of the original.

Excellent served in a falafel wrap (obviously!), but also good in all manner of sandwiches.

3 turnips (about 600 g/1 lb. 5 oz.), scrubbed if they're looking dirty

1 large beetroot/beet (about 150–200 g/5–7 oz.)

2 garlic cloves, peeled and lightly crushed

1 red chilli/chile

150 ml/²/₃ cup white vinegar

25 g/1 oz. white sugar

25 g/1 oz. salt

2 dried bay leaves

1 teaspoon black peppercorns

¹/₂ teaspoon sumac

Makes 1 large jar (unless your turnips are monsters)

Cut the turnips into fat matchsticks or chips and place in a large bowl. Peel and grate the beetroot directly into the same bowl (gloves are useful here to prevent your hands being stained pink). Using a metal spoon, stir to make sure the vegetables are well mixed together. Add the garlic cloves, which should be lightly crushed. Take the red chilli and pierce it a couple of times with the tip of a knife. Add this to the bowl and toss to mix.

Add all of the mixed vegetables to a sterilized jar.

In the same bowl (no need to wash it out), mix the vinegar with 250 ml/1 cup water, along with the sugar and salt. Whisk vigorously until the sugar and salt dissolve and the brine clears. Add the bay Leaves, black peppercorns and sumac and whisk again gently.

Pour the brine over the vegetables, seal the jar and give it a shake to mix everything together.

The turnips will gradually pick up the colour from the beetroot, going a lovely pink colour. This should take about a week, but the pickles will be tasty sooner than that. They'll keep for at least one month when stored in the fridge.

Spicy pickled radishes

In Korea, a particularly popular way of preparing pickled daikon (or mooli) is known as 'chicken mu' because these salty, sweet pickles go so well with the country's incredible fried chicken.

Daikon isn't super easy to get hold of unless you live near a decent Asian supermarket, so we've adapted the recipe to work with breakfast radishes, which are easier to find.

Whichever type of radish you use, this is 100% the pickle to serve the next time you have fried chicken in any format. Obviously, they go brilliantly with Korean-style fried chicken, but we've successfully added a couple of these pickles to a bucket of the Colonel's finest with good results.

20 breakfast radishes
(about 500 g/1 lb. 2 oz.)

15 g/^{1}/$_2$ oz. salt

250 ml/1 cup rice vinegar

2 tablespoons soy sauce

^{1}/$_2$ tablespoon Korean gochugaru chilli/chile flakes (see Note for alternatives)

75 g/^{1}/$_3$ cup white sugar

3 garlic cloves, thinly sliced

Makes 1 medium jar

Give the radishes a thorough rinse under cold water and drain. When dry, cut the tops and stringy bottoms off the radishes but otherwise leave them whole (unless you find yourself dealing with particularly large radishes, which may need cutting in half).

Add to a bowl, tip in the salt and toss vigorously to combine. Continue to agitate the radishes in the bowl until they start to give up some of their water. Cover the bowl and set aside for 4 hours. During this period the radishes should release a decent amount of water.

After 4 hours, tip the radishes into a colander/strainer in the sink to drain, then rinse with cold water. Place the salted radishes in a sterilized jar.

Add the rice vinegar and 100 ml/scant ^{1}/$_2$ cup water to a saucepan with the soy sauce, gochugaru flakes and sugar. Add the sliced garlic to the brine. Bring to the boil, stirring to make sure the sugar is completely dissolved.

Allow the brine to cool completely, then pour over the radishes, ensuring they are completely submerged. Seal the jar and store in the fridge.

These pickles need a bit of time to mature, so they'll be ready to eat after 5 days and last one month when stored in the fridge.

A NOTE ON GOCHUGARU

Gochugaru is a dried chilli/chile flake used extensively throughout Korean cooking. It has a smoky flavour with a mild heat and we get through loads while making kimchi. It can be hard to track down, but can usually be found in larger Asian supermarkets. If you can't find any, dried chilli/red pepper flakes, paprika or Turkish pul biber (also called Aleppo chilli sometimes) can be substituted.

Instant pickled tomato and cucumber salad

This recipe is so simple it almost feels like a cheat, but the results are absolutely incredible. It perfectly showcases how the quick pickle technique of just adding salt and sugar to vegetables, then giving them a moment for flavour to develop, really delivers taste results way beyond the effort you put in.

If we're being honest about it, a version of this pickle is probably the pickle we make the most at home. It goes alongside everything from a sabich (see page 116) to a pickled shawarma. We've even been known to make this quickly after ordering a takeaway kebab/kabob because it really is no effort and is so much nicer than the sweaty box of limp vegetables that inevitably arrive with even the best kebab.

2 medium tomatoes

1 large cucumber

$\frac{1}{2}$ red onion

1 tablespoon salt

1 teaspoon white sugar

1 teaspoon sumac

juice of 1 lemon

1 tablespoon olive oil

a large handful of flat-leaf parsley

Serves 4 as a side

Chop the tomatoes into 1-cm/$\frac{1}{2}$-inch cubes and add to a bowl. Cut the cucumber in half and use a teaspoon to remove the seeds. Cut the remaining flesh into cubes of a similar size to the tomatoes and add to the bowl. Slice the red onion as thinly as you can and mix with the tomatoes and cucumbers.

Add the salt and sugar and toss vigorously to combine. Add the sumac and toss once more. Set aside for 30 minutes to let the salt draw out some of the water from the vegetables.

After 30 minutes, drain the brine that has been released by the vegetables into a separate bowl. Mix with the lemon juice and the olive oil to make a sharp dressing.

Roughly chop the parsley and stir through the vegetables. When ready to eat, give the dressing a final whisk and pour over the vegetables. Toss so they are all coated and serve as a side.

As this is a quick pickle that uses mostly soft vegetables, it doesn't last long at all. We're talking just a couple of hours before everything becomes mushy and unpalatable. But it's also such a doddle to make, you should be able to knock it up anytime you need a lightly pickled side.

'Don't call it kimchi' lacto-fermented Chinese leaf cabbage

Shedletskys really started with kimchi. We hosted a dinner party in our tiny Dalston flat in 2012 where we cooked a feast. As part of the meal, we made our own kimchi. And that, as they say, was that. We started hosting regular pop-ups and refined and adapted our recipe for making kimchi over the next few years. Today at Shedletskys, we make thousands of jars a month and have won awards for our interpretation. This isn't that recipe though. Shedletskys' kimchi is naturally fermented and deliberately simple in terms of flavourings. We want to let the tang and funk develop on its own, so it's a slow process. It's not uncommon for us to ferment batches for a month before we're happy with it.

So for the home cook, we've changed things up a bit. We still salt the cabbage to start things off, but the paste that flavours the kimchi uses vinegar, so this is much closer to a pickle than a traditional fermented kimchi. It means it's ready to eat in just a couple of days and has a recognizably kimchi-y flavour profile, although it would probably upset traditionalists and gets a bit slimy and unpleasant if stored for more than a couple of weeks.

1 Chinese leaf cabbage (about 650 g/ 1 lb. 7 oz.), sliced into quarters, then into 3-cm/1¼-inch slices

20 g/¾ oz. salt (approximate amount – see recipe)

1 large carrot, peeled and sliced into 5-cm/2-inch matchsticks

150 g/5½ oz. daikon (or any radish you have on hand), peeled and sliced into 5-cm/2-inch matchsticks

1 conference pear, peeled, quartered and cored, then cut into 2-3-mm/ ⅛-inch slices

1 red chilli/chile, halved, deseeded and thinly sliced

3 spring onions/scallions, thinly sliced

a thumb-sized piece of fresh ginger, peeled and thinly sliced

4 garlic cloves, peeled and thinly sliced

50 g/1¾ oz. Korean gochugaru chilli/ chile flakes (see Note on page 50)

50 g/1¾ oz. white sugar

6 tablespoons fish sauce

4 tablespoons rice vinegar

Makes 1 large jar

Weigh the sliced cabbage, then add it to a large bowl.

For the amount of salt, calculate 3% of the weight of the cabbage (see Bread and Butter Pickles, page 58) and add that amount of salt to the bowl. Massage the cabbage gently until it starts to release some water. At this point, cover the bowl and set aside for at least 4 hours or ideally overnight. Once the cabbage has been salted, rinse well in cold water, then drain. Return the cabbage to the bowl.

Add the carrot, daikon, pear, chilli and spring onions to the cabbage bowl. Give everything a final mix and let it sit while you make the brine paste.

Add the ginger and garlic to a clean bowl. Add the gochugaru flakes, sugar, fish sauce and rice wine vinegar. Stir them together until a paste forms. If it's too thick, add a scant teaspoon of water. You're looking for something that's the consistency of double/heavy cream.

Scrape the paste into the cabbage mixture and stir until everything is very well combined. You want to make sure all the vegetables are completely coated in the paste. Using your hands to massage everything together is messy but the best approach.

Press the kimchi mixture into a large sterilized jar and weigh down the vegetables with a fermentation weight or water-filled, sealable plastic sandwich bag. Set aside for 24 hours. In that time, more liquid will leech from the vegetables. After 24 hours, stir once again and store in the fridge. Wait 24 more hours before consuming and use within a couple of weeks.

'Curtido' South American pickled cabbage

Despite both my heritage and our collective love of Eastern European and deli foods, neither Nat nor I have really got on very well with making our own sauerkraut. We always claim that it's because, in its purest form, there's not too much room to play around with this particular ferment. And while that is true to some extent, it's also true that, like homemade mayonnaise, sauerkraut is a bit of a culinary bête noir *for us. However carefully we weigh things; however long we spend massaging the cabbage; and however carefully we ensure the vegetables are covered by the brine, our sauerkraut simply never comes out *that* tasty. I mean it's usually fine, but even our best batches probably aren't really any better than the stuff you can get in jars from a Polish deli. Plus, we usually have a couple of jars of curtido lying around. This Salvadorian pickle is delicious in its own right. Like sauerkraut, it's a little bit funky and sour from the fermentation, but its flavour profile gets taken up a notch with a big hit of Mexican oregano, lime juice and chilli.*

1 large white cabbage
(about 750 g/1 lb. 10 oz.)

40–50 g/1½–2 oz. salt (approximate amount – see recipe and Note)

2 white onions, peeled, halved and thinly sliced

1 large carrot, peeled and cut into matchsticks

5 garlic cloves, peeled and thinly sliced

1 red chilli/chile, thinly sliced

2 tablespoons Mexican oregano (use regular oregano if you can't find the more floral Mexican variety)

finely grated zest and juice of 5 limes

100 ml/⅓ cup plus 1 tablespoon white vinegar

Makes 1 large jar

A NOTE ON WEIGHTS

These aren't technically fermented as they go into a very acidic pickle brine long before any fermentation can realistically occur, but they do get a salting ahead of the pickling stage, so weighing things is important.

Cut the cabbage into quarters and remove any outer leaves that don't look appealing. Cut out the woody core, then slice the cabbage very thinly. This is best achieved by putting the cabbage quarters through the slicing blade on a food processor or using a mandolin: it can also be done by hand, if necessary. Weigh the sliced cabbage, then add it to a large bowl. For the amount of salt, calculate 5% of the weight of the cabbage. (We use 40 g/1½ oz. salt for 800 g/1¾ lb. cabbage.)

Using your hands, massage the salt into the cabbage. Keep massaging until all the cabbage is very well coated and it's starting to release some of its moisture. Set aside while you prepare your other vegetables, a matter of 10–15 minutes.

Add the onion and carrot to the cabbage mixture and toss again. Add the garlic, chilli, Mexican oregano and lime zest. Now, roll your sleeves up and really give the cabbage a serious knead. Press and massage the vegetables against the side of the bowl. You're aiming to really break down the cabbage and for it to release a lot of water (potentially enough to completely cover the vegetables, although this isn't always possible in the bowl).

After a few minutes of kneading, transfer the vegetables into a large sterilized jar. Continue to mix and muddle the cabbage as you put it into the jar and cover with any liquid left in the mixing bowl. Pour the lime juice and vinegar over the top of the vegetables. Weigh down all the vegetables so they are completely submerged using a fermentation weight or a water-filled, sealable plastic sandwich bag. Cover the bowl and set aside.

The pickle will be ready after a few hours, but even better after a few days. After about a week, place in the fridge to prevent further fermentation. Stored in the fridge, this will be good for at least 6 weeks and probably longer.

Bread and butter pickles

A version of these pickles has been a Shedletskys staple since the earliest days of the business. And from our first ever market stall, we've been asked the same question: 'Why are these called "bread and butter" pickles?' We've always given the answer that they are a product of the Great Depression. The story goes that during the 1930s in the USA, people were so poor they often had sandwiches with just a smear of butter and a few of these pickles between two slices of bread.

These pickles – fairly unique in that the cucumbers are cooked for longer than normal in their brine – are tasty enough to be enjoyed in a sandwich on their own. But of course, they don't have to be consumed so plainly. They are equally good with a burger, or in basically any sandwich. This brine and spice mix is fantastic and is the basis for many of the other recipes in this book.

700 g/1 lb. 7 oz. cucumber (about 6 pickling cucumbers or a couple of 'normal' salad cucumbers)

20 g/³/₄ oz. salt (approximate amount – see recipe)

10 g/¹/₃ oz. white sugar (approximate amount – see recipe)

1 white onion, halved and thinly sliced

BRINE

500 ml/2 cups white vinegar

150 g/³/₄ cup white sugar

75 g/¹/₄ cup plus 2 tablespoons brown sugar

a thumb-sized piece of fresh turmeric root (use 10 g/¹/₃ oz. of ground turmeric if fresh is unavailable), peeled and sliced into matchsticks

BREAD AND BUTTER SPICE MIX

1 teaspoon black peppercorns

¹/₂ tablespoon cumin seeds

¹/₂ tablespoon coriander seeds

pinch of whole cloves (about 3–4 cloves)

1 teaspoon fenugreek seeds

3 cardamom pods

1 tablespoon yellow mustard seeds

Makes 1 medium jar

Top and tail the cucumbers, then slice into 2–3 mm/¹/₈-inch rounds. Once all the cucumbers are chopped, weigh the resulting slices and make a note. Add 3% of the total weight of the cucumbers in salt and 1.5% in sugar.

To calculate this, take the weight of cucumbers in grams and divide that by 100. Then multiple the resulting number by 3 and 1.5 to get the quantities of salt and sugar respectively. In our case, we ended up with 638 g of sliced cucumbers. So we added 19 g/³/₄ oz. salt ((683÷100)x3=19.19 rounded down to 19) and 10 g/¹/₃ oz. of sugar ((683÷100)x1.5=9.6 rounded up to 10).

Stir the salt and sugar into the cucumbers well. The vegetables should start to release some of their water while you do this. Cover and set aside for 2 hours.

After a couple of hours, drain the cucumbers in a fine sieve/strainer. Rinse under cold running water and allow to drain in the sink while you prepare the hot brine.

To make the brine, add the vinegar to a large saucepan and heat over a medium heat. Add both the sugars and stir to dissolve. Add the turmeric, along with the spice mix. If using ground turmeric, stir it into the brine now.

Bring the brine to the boil. Once boiling, carefully add the cucumbers and onions and stir so they are all mixed together and submerged in the brine. Return to the boil and cook for 3–5 minutes until the cucumbers have darkened considerably and the onions are soft and yellow.

Using a slotted spoon, transfer the vegetables to a sterilized jar. Bring the brine back to the boil and pour over the vegetables. Seal the jar and allow to cool completely before eating, or store in the fridge for up to one month.

Pickled green tomatoes

One of the real joys of pickling is how it gives you a great excuse to buy vegetables even when you're not 100% sure you know what you're going to do with them. You can be relatively certain that even if they don't slot into your normal cooking routine, you can always pickle them and end up with something delicious.

That's how this recipe came about. We spotted an appealing looking pile of green tomatoes in our local Turkish supermarket, bought a load and took them home. A search of our cookbook collection didn't turn up many recipe options that we fancied, so we decided to pickle them. (As a side note, is there anything you can do with these fruits that isn't a variation on Fried Green Tomatoes?) The results were fantastic. Time in the brine softened the tough skin of the tomatoes and gave a much-needed boost to what was actually a bit of a one-note sour flavour. Thinly sliced, these pickles have become a sandwich staple and are fantastic for adding zing to a burger.

1 kg/2¼ lb. firm green tomatoes with stalks

4 garlic cloves

1 red chilli/chile

5 fresh thyme sprigs

500 ml/2 cups white vinegar

50 g/¼ cup white sugar

30 g/2 tablespoons salt

1 teaspoon black peppercorns

1 teaspoon yellow mustard seeds

Makes 1 large jar

Remove the stalks from the tomatoes and reserve for later. Give the tomatoes themselves a thorough wash and allow to dry. Halve each tomato. Peel and lightly crush the garlic cloves and pierce the red chilli a couple of times with the tip of a sharp knife. Add them all to a large sterilized jar, along with the reserved tomato stalks and all of the thyme.

Make a brine by mixing 500 ml/2 cups water and the vinegar with the sugar and salt. Bring to the boil over a medium heat, stirring until the sugar and salt have completely dissolved. Add the black peppercorns and mustard seeds, then pour the hot brine directly over the tomatoes. Allow to cool slightly before sealing the jar.

Store in the fridge for at least a week before eating. These will be good for up to 6 weeks when stored in the fridge.

Pickled cherries

Nat is a big fan of blintzes – the thin filled pancakes traditionally eaten around Shavuot. A favourite way to eat them is with a sweetened cheese filling and a lightly cooked cherry compote. One day, instead of making the compote, Nat suggested pickling the cherries; it was a revelation.

The tart fruit in a sweeter-than-normal brine are brilliant with the filled pancakes. But they are also delicious in all manner of salads and sandwiches. They even work with other stronger cheeses as a condiment.

Just a quick note, we leave the stones/pits in the cherries before we pickle them because we think the stones add an interesting, subtle almondy note to the brine. However, it does mean you have to pit them once pickled, which can be a bit messy. If you're so inclined, remove and discard the cherry stones before pickling. You'll lose a bit of flavour, but you'll be repaid with an easier-to-eat pickle. You could also try adding the reserved stones to the brine separately, but just be careful you don't accidentally try to eat one once pickled.

500 g/1 lb. 2 oz. ripe cherries, stones/pits left in
600 ml/2$\frac{1}{2}$ cups cider vinegar
200 g/1 cup white sugar
75 g/2$\frac{3}{4}$ oz. salt
$\frac{1}{2}$ teaspoon whole cloves
$\frac{1}{2}$ teaspoon coriander seeds
1 whole star anise
1 teaspoon pink peppercorns
$\frac{1}{2}$ teaspoon whole allspice (pimento berries)

Makes 1 medium jar

Wash the cherries and remove most of the stalks. If you want to remove the stones, now's the time. Keep the cherries as intact as possible while pitting them, so preferably use a handheld cherry pitter. Add the prepared cherries to a sterilized jar.

Make a brine by combining the vinegar with sugar and salt and bringing to the boil over a medium heat. Keep stirring to dissolve everything.

Meanwhile, add the whole spices to a dry frying pan/skillet and warm over a medium heat for about 3 minutes or until they are very lightly toasted.

Add the toasted spices to the brine, then pour directly over the cherries. Allow to cool before sealing the jar and storing in the fridge.

The cherries will be ready to eat after 5 days and last for up to a couple of months when stored in the fridge.

Cooking
with Pickles

Pickle-packed latkes
with pickle-brine apple sauce and sour cream

Traditionally potato latkes are eaten around Chanukah with either apple sauce
OR sour cream, but more often than not we consume ours with BOTH sauces.
In a further blow to tradition, we spike our latkes heavily with pickles and pep
our apple sauce with a whack of pickle brine to give it a bit more oomph.

PICKLE-BRINE APPLE SAUCE

4 medium Granny Smith apples (or any other tart green apples)

juice of 1 lemon

150 ml/²/₃ cup Bread and Butter Pickles brine, plus more to taste (see page 58)

25 g/1 heaped tablespoon white sugar

salt and freshly ground black pepper

LATKES

500 g/18 oz. Maris Piper potatoes

1 white onion (about 100 g/3¹/₂ oz.)

150 g/5¹/₂ oz. Bread and Butter Pickles (see page 58), drained and roughly chopped

2 eggs, beaten

50 g/¹/₃ cup fine matzo meal

vegetable oil, for frying

TO SERVE

sour cream

Makes 6 large latkes
or enough for 2 greedy people

First, make the apple sauce. Start by peeling, coring and finely slicing the apples. Add them to a small saucepan and toss with the lemon juice as you go to prevent the apples discolouring. When all the apples are prepared, add the pickle brine and sugar. Warm over a medium heat, stirring occasionally, for about 10 minutes until the apples break down to a chunky sauce.

Taste and adjust the seasoning with salt and pepper and leave to cool. At this point you can leave the apple sauce chunky, if you want, or add the sauce to a blender and blitz to a smooth purée. Whichever you choose, store the apple sauce in a container in the fridge while you make the latkes.

To make the latkes, peel and grate the potatoes using the large holes on a box grater. Take a clean dish towel and use it to line a large bowl. Add the grated potatoes to the lined bowl and draw up the corners of the towel to make a ball. Squeeze and twist tightly over the bowl to extract as much water as possible. When the potatoes are squeezed dry, discard the water that has gathered in the bowl, but leave the white potato starch that will have settled at the bottom. Tip the now dry potatoes into the bowl with the potato starch.

Peel and grate the onion with the grater used for the potatoes directly into the potatoes. Add the chopped Bread and Butter Pickles and the eggs to the potato and onion mix, then stir to combine. Add the matzo meal, season with salt and black pepper and mix again. Cover the bowl and set aside in the fridge for 30 minutes.

Heat a couple of teaspoons of vegetable oil in a large frying pan/skillet set over a medium heat. Remove the latke mixture from the fridge and use a large spoon to make 6 patties of equal size.

When the oil is hot, gently place the patties into the pan and cook undisturbed for 5 minutes until one side is golden brown. Press down, then carefully flip and cook the other side for a further 5 minutes. Pay close attention to the temperature and adjust the heat if the latkes are browning too quickly. Flip again and cook for a further 3 minutes, or until golden brown on both sides. Remove from the pan and drain on paper towels.

Serve warm with the apple sauce and a large dollop of sour cream.

Deep-fried pickles with ranch dressing

We wanted to do something different from the classic deep-fried pickles. And because we're super happy with the cornmeal-based batter used in our hush puppy recipe (in fact one American diner at a recent pop-up told us they were the best she'd ever had), we thought it would be fun to have a go at making corn dogs with pickles in place of the hot dogs.

The real skill comes in coating the pickles completely in the batter and getting them into the hot oil without losing the total coverage. You can just drop slices of pickles into the batter – you'll get what amounts to pickle-stuffed hush puppies, and that's never a bad thing.

RANCH DIP

80 ml/¹/₃ cup buttermilk

150 ml/²/₃ cup mayonnaise

50 ml/3½ tablespoons reserved pickle brine

juice of ¹/₂ lemon

¹/₂ teaspoon onion powder

¹/₂ teaspoon garlic powder

2 tablespoons chopped fresh dill

2 tablespoons snipped fresh chives

salt and freshly ground black pepper

DEEP-FRIED PICKLES

1 large jar whole pickled gherkins, drained and brine reserved

100 g/³/₄ cup self-raising/rising flour

100 g/³/₄ cup corn flour/cornmeal

50 g/heaped ¹/₃ cup plain/ all-purpose flour

4 teaspoons salt

1 teaspoon white sugar

¹/₂ teaspoon bicarbonate of/ baking soda

¹/₂ teaspoon baking powder

25 g/1 oz. pickled chillies/chiles (optional)

1 large/US extra-large egg

65 g/¹/₄ cup whole/full-fat milk

125 g/¹/₂ cup reserved pickled brine

vegetable oil, for deep frying

kebab/kabob skewers

Serves 4 as a snack

First, drain the gherkins and reserve the brine and the jar.

Next, make the ranch dip. Mix together the buttermilk, mayonnaise, reserved pickle brine and lemon juice in a bowl. Add the onion powder and garlic powder, then stir to combine. Add the herbs to the dip, then taste and adjust the seasoning with salt and pepper as needed.

In a large bowl, mix together all of the dry ingredients for the batter with a whisk. When well mixed, add the pickled chillies, if using.

In a separate smaller bowl, beat together the egg, milk and reserved pickle brine. Whisk the wet ingredients into the dry mix and stir to combine. Decant the batter into the reserved pickle jar.

Fill a deep-fat fryer to the fill line with oil and heat to 180°C/350°F. Alternatively, half-fill a heavy high-sided saucepan with oil and carefully heat on the hob/ stovetop. Use a thermometer to check the temperature.

While keeping a close eye on the oil as it heats, skewer each pickle with a kebab/kabob skewer.

As soon as the oil is hot enough, working in batches, add the skewered pickles to the jar full of batter and twizzle each one so they are completely coated. Quickly, but carefully, lower them into the oil, leaving the exposed part of the skewer out of the oil.

Deep-fry the pickles until they float to the surface of the oil, then turn gently. Fry for 5–7 minutes, turning occasionally, until the batter is a uniform deep brown. Using a slotted spoon, remove the pickles from the oil and drain on paper towels or a wire rack to remove any excess oil. Serve this freshly cooked batch of pickles with the ranch dip while you coat and fry the next batch.

NOTE

Any batter left at the end can be cooked on its own. Simply use an ice-cream scoop to drop balls of batter into the hot oil and cook for 6–7 minutes until deeply brown.

Pickle-brine chicken wings with blue cheese dip

The lockdowns during the COVID-19 pandemic, forced us to turn our house into a full-scale pickle factory. As well as making hundreds of jars of kimchi and pickles in our dining room, we ran what turned out to be a pretty successful meal kit service. Each week, we cooked and delivered up to one hundred 'Make Away' boxes across London, all produced with just a couple of domestic ovens.

These chicken wings were one of our bestselling items – a perennial favourite that happily helped us make use of the excess pickle brine that filled our living room at the time. The combination of buttermilk and pickle brine in the marinade results in a wing that's extremely tender, a lovely contrast to the crispy coating.

CHICKEN WINGS

150 ml/²/₃ cup buttermilk

250 ml/1 cup pickle brine (we use Bread and Butter Pickles brine on page 58, but use whatever brine you have. If you don't have enough brine to hand, let down whatever you do have with equal parts water and vinegar)

2 teaspoons salt

1 tablespoon any hot sauce (see Note), plus extra to serve

freshly ground black pepper

1 kg/2¼ lb. chicken wings

100 g/¾ cup plain/all-purpose flour

100 g/¾ cup corn flour/cornmeal

1 tablespoon Bread and Butter Spice Mix (see page 58)

vegetable oil, for deep frying

BLUE CHEESE DIP

150 g/5½ oz. blue cheese, crumbled

100 g/3½ oz. mayonnaise

50 ml/¼ cup sour cream

1 tablespoon pickle brine

squeeze of lemon juice

freshly ground black pepper

Serves 4 as an appetizer

In a plastic container that will fit all the wings, make the marinade. Mix together the buttermilk and pickle brine with the salt and hot sauce. Season with plenty of black pepper. Add the chicken wings and toss until well coated. Seal the container and refrigerate for at least one hour and up to 4 hours.

While the wings are marinating, make the blue cheese dip. Place all of the ingredients, except the lemon juice, in the bowl of a food processor and pulse to a smooth consistency. Season with lemon juice and plenty of black pepper.

When ready to cook the wings, fill a deep-fat fryer to the fill line with oil and heat to 160°C/325°F. Alternatively, half-fill a heavy high-sided saucepan with oil and carefully heat on the hob/stovetop. Use a thermometer to check the temperature.

Make a dredge by mixing the flour and corn flour in a bowl with the Bread and Butter Spice Mix and season with salt and pepper.

When you're ready to start frying, heat the oven to 120°C/100°C fan/225°F/Gas ¼ or its lowest setting and line a baking sheet with paper towels.

Working in batches, take the wings out of the marinade, allowing any excess marinade to drip off, then drop them into the seasoned flour. Toss the wings in the flour to coat, then immediately (and carefully) lower them into the hot oil. Deep-fry the chicken wings for 10 minutes until golden brown and an instant read thermometer inserted into the thickest part of a wing shows 74°C/165°F. Transfer the wings to the lined baking sheet to drain, then keep warm in a low oven while you coat and fry the remaining wings.

When all the wings are fried, add to a bowl and season with more salt. Add 50 ml/3½ tablespoons hot sauce and toss to coat. Serve immediately with the dip.

NOTE ON HOT SAUCE

We coat these wings in our Pickleback Hot Sauce (that can be bought from our website) to really dial up their pickley-ness, but you can use any hot sauce. Try the Pickle Brine Hot Sauce on page 133 if you want to make your own.

Pickle party platter with dips

A great way to start a meal is with a big ol' plate of pickles and lovely dips. Gather whatever pickles you have, make one, two or all three of these delicious dips and prepare to enjoy a proper pickle party.

PLAIN LABNEH

1 kg/2¼ lb. best-quality full-fat yogurt (we use the 14% stuff from a brand called 'Yayla' when we can get it)

2 tablespoons sea salt

olive oil, to serve

a large piece of muslin/cheesecloth or a clean dish towel

a small piece of string

SESAME AUBERGINE DIP

3 aubergines/eggplants

a whole head of garlic

2 tablespoons sesame oil

2 teaspoons soy sauce

½ teaspoon Korean gochugaru chilli/chile flakes (see Note on page 50)

a drop of liquid smoke (optional)

1 tablespoon rice vinegar

PICKLE-BRINE TAHINI DIP

250 g/1 cup best-quality tahini

juice of 1 lemon

½ teaspoon salt

100 ml/⅓ cup pickle brine

TO ASSEMBLE

a selection of handmade pickles

fresh crunchy veg, cut into crudités (like the best 1970s dinner party)

crackers and potato crisps/chips

Serves 4–6

To make the labneh, mix the salt into the yogurt. Lay a piece of muslin or a clean dish towel in a colander/strainer and spoon the yogurt into the middle. Bring the four corners together to make a tight ball with the yogurt inside. Twist the top to make it as tight as you can and tie with string. Place the colander in large bowl to drain and transfer to the fridge The longer you leave the yogurt the thicker the labneh will be. The minimum is 6 hours for a lighter dip. We often leave the yogurt for 24 hours until it achieves an almost goat cheese-esque texture. When you're happy with the consistency, gently undo the ball and transfer the labneh to a container. Pour olive oil over the top to cover and store in the fridge until needed.

To make the aubergine dip, switch the oven to the highest grill/broiler setting. Place the aubergines on a baking sheet and grill, turning every 10 minutes, until cooked through and the skin is blistered and charred. This should take about 30 minutes depending on how hot the grill is. They're done when the aubergines are completely soft and collapsing. Remove the aubergines from the oven and tip into a bowl. Cover tightly with cling film/plastic wrap and let cool slightly. Meanwhile, preheat the oven to 180°C/160°C fan/350°F/Gas 4 and wrap the garlic in foil. Bake for 30 minutes until soft. Remove from the oven to cool.

When cool enough to handle, carefully peel the aubergines, placing the flesh in a food processor. Squeeze in the garlic and add the sesame oil, soy sauce, gochugaru flakes, rice vinegar and liquid smoke (if using). Blend to a smooth purée. Adjust the seasoning with salt and sesame oil, if necessary. Store in the fridge until needed.

For the tahini dip, combine the tahini, lemon juice and salt in a bowl. Gradually whisk in the pickle brine, stirring continuously until a thick sauce forms. It may initially look like it's split but keep whisking and the sauce will come back together. Add the brine in increments so you can assess the consistency. Store in the fridge until ready to serve.

To serve, drain the brine from your chosen pickles and arrange on a platter. Decant the dips into serving bowls and add to the platter with little piles of crudités. Dress the dips with a drizzle of olive oil and maybe some chilli flakes, herbs and salt. Encourage everyone to dive in.

A NOTE ABOUT LABNEH

We keep our labneh pretty plain with just salt, but feel free to experiment with other flavours. A tablespoon of lemon zest stirred through before straining is lovely, as is a generous pinch of sumac. Fresh herbs like chives or dill also work a treat. Try the plain version first and then have a play.

Chicken skin with pickle dust

The hardest part of this recipe is probably managing to save enough chicken skin to make the slow-cooking process worthwhile. Once you have the skin, all you need is the patience to carefully render out the fat and create these little crispy bites that are almost definitely superior to their distinctly unkosher cousins – the pork scratching.

We usually save the skin when using chicken pieces to make curries. Or try to keep as much skin as possible if we use a whole bird for chicken soup. The pieces of skin can be stored in the freezer in a sandwich bag while you build up enough. Then it's simply a matter of defrosting it thoroughly before starting the recipe.

These crispy nuggets are an excellent vehicle for showing off any pickle dust you have lying around, so have a play and season with any flavours you fancy.

500 g/1 lb. 2 oz. chicken skin (thawed, if frozen)

1 teaspoon salt, plus extra for seasoning

2 teaspoons Dried Pickle Dust (see page 134) – we've used Bread and Butter Pickles on page 58 and Pink Pickled Turnips on page 49 to make this dust to great effect

Makes enough for a snack for 4 people (or 2 greedy people)

First, pat the chicken skins dry with paper towels, then cut into strips. You want them all to be about 1-cm/$^{1}/_{2}$-inch wide but the length will vary depending on the bits of skin you have managed to collect.

Place the pieces of skin into a cold, large cast-iron skillet (or non-stick frying pan) with a splash of water and warm over a low heat on the hob/stovetop. Add the salt and stir to mix.

Bring the heat up and continue to cook the skins over a medium heat, stirring regularly. Over the next 25–30 minutes, any water will evaporate and the skins will extrude their schmaltz. Keep cooking and stirring. Be patient. Let time pass. Think about how delicious the crispy bits of fat will be when they're ready. Eventually the skin will start to turn brown and curl up.

After about 40 minutes the skins will be light brown all over and begin to look crispy. At this point, remove the pan from the heat and strain off the fat through a fine mesh sieve/strainer. Leave this to cool and save the fat for something else (making kneidlach for matzo ball soup, for example).

Back to the business at hand.

Return the skin to the pan and add a little bit more salt. Heat again over a medium heat, stirring very regularly, until the skin is deep brown and very crisp. This should take a further 10–15 minutes. Pay attention to the heat level and cooking process and adjust if it feels like the skin is burning.

Remove the now crispy skin from the pan and drain on paper towels. Add to a serving bowl and sprinkle with Pickle Dust. Toss to coat and eat immediately.

Pickled beetroot borscht

When you've got a big jar of our pickled beetroot (see page 46) in the fridge, making this classic soup is a doddle. And even if you don't have a jar to hand, shop-bought pickled beetroot works almost as well.

There are probably as many versions of borscht as there are Eastern European grandmas out there. Ours dials up the sweet/sour notes with lots of pickle brine to complement the earthy beetroot. We serve it as a silky smooth soup because that's how James prefers it, but you could forgo the final blend and leave it chunky, if you want. What we would say is that this is a borscht that benefits from being served warm, rather than – as is perhaps more traditional – chilled. Served cold, this is just a little close to a big bowl of pickles. Even for us, that's a bit much.

1 tablespoon vegetable oil

1 large onion, roughly chopped

4 carrots, peeled and roughly chopped

2 celery sticks/ribs, roughly chopped

1 large potato, peeled and roughly chopped

600 g/1 lb. 5 oz. Borscht-style Pickled Beetroot (see page 46)

400 ml/1¾ cups pickle brine

850 ml/3½ cups stock (beef stock to be traditional, but any will work)

juice of 1 lemon

salt and freshly ground black pepper

TO SERVE

sour cream

finely chopped fresh dill

Serves 4

Add the oil to a heavy-based saucepan and warm over a medium heat. Add the onion and sweat gently for a couple of minutes, before adding the carrot, celery and potato. Cook all the vegetables over a gentle heat for about 15 minutes until soft, being careful not to colour them too much in the process.

Drain the pickled beetroot, reserving the brine for later. Roughly chop the beetroot and add to the pan, along with some of the pickling spices from the jar. Cook down the beetroot for a couple of minutes before adding the reserved pickle brine (if necessary, add enough water to make it up to 400 ml/1⅔ cups) and 750 ml/3 cups of the stock. Season with salt. Bring to a simmer and cook for 45 minutes, or until the beetroot is very soft.

Leave the beetroot to cool slightly. Remove any bay leaves that might have snuck in from the pickle brine. Transfer the beetroot to a blender and blitz until very smooth. If the soup feels a bit thick, adjust the consistency with additional stock or water. We ended up adding another 100 ml/scant ½ cup of stock to make a velvety pink soup.

Return the soup to a clean saucepan and heat gently. Taste and adjust the seasoning. It will need lots of black pepper and lemon juice and may need a little extra salt (or even a tiny pinch of sugar) depending on the brine that was used. Serve the soup ladled into deep bowls with a big swirl of sour cream and lots of finely chopped dill.

NOTE

If you plan on blending the soup later on, don't worry too much about the neatness of your chopping when preparing the vegetables, but if you want to leave the soup chunky, take a bit more care to chop everything evenly.

Kentucky roast lamb with black brine 'mop' sauce

The original tagline for Shedletskys was going to be 'Salt, Smoke and Schmaltz'. During our BBQ-ing heyday we devoured cookbooks from the US dedicated to the art. In one we came across a recipe for a smoked lamb from Kentucky that used a vinegar-based marinade applied during the cooking process. When we saw that recipe for a sweet, vinegary sauce served with lamb, we immediately thought of the British tradition of serving mint sauce with lamb. So we've adapted the recipe to take it more in this direction, but with added pickle brine of course!

½ leg of bone-in lamb (weighing about 1.2 kg/2¾ lb.)

2 tablespoons salt

'MOP' SAUCE

50-g/1¾-oz. can or jar anchovy fillets in oil

1 tablespoon Worcestershire sauce

1 teaspoon dark soy sauce

200 ml/scant 1 cup pickle brine

80 ml/⅓ cup white vinegar

6 tablespoons brown sugar

½ teaspoon dried mint

¼ teaspoon onion powder

3 garlic cloves, peeled and lightly crushed

LAMB RUB

½ teaspoon black peppercorns

½ teaspoon mustard seeds

1 teaspoon coriander seeds

1 teaspoon cumin seeds

½ teaspoon fennel seeds

¼ teaspoon dried chilli/ hot red pepper flakes

1 tablespoon fresh thyme leaves

1 tablespoon vegetable oil

TO FINISH THE SAUCE

bunch of fresh mint, leaves chopped

2 tablespoons butter

Serves 4 as a main plate
(Double the quantities to feed more with a whole leg of lamb)

Place the lamb in a large airtight container and salt generously, turning the lamb to make sure it is well coated. Put the lid on and refrigerate overnight. The next morning, remove the lamb from the fridge and preheat the oven to 120°C/100°C fan/250°F/Gas ½.

To make the 'mop' sauce, heat a small saucepan over a medium heat and add the anchovies and the oil from the can or jar. Cook, stirring regularly, until the anchovies have broken down into a paste. Add the Worcestershire sauce, dark soy sauce, pickle brine, white vinegar, brown sugar, dried mint, onion powder and 250 ml/1 cup water and mix. Add the garlic, then bring to the boil and bubble vigorously for 10 minutes. Remove from the heat and leave to cool slightly before straining through a fine-mesh sieve/strainer into a clean bowl.

Grind all the spices and herbs for the rub together either in an electric spice grinder or using a pestle and mortar. Tip the mixture into a small bowl and add the oil to make a thick paste.

Place the lamb on a lipped baking sheet and liberally apply the rub on all sides of the lamb. Roast in the oven for 1 hour, then paint a coating of the 'mop' sauce over the lamb and return to the oven. Cook for 7 more hours, basting with the sauce every hour or so.

After 8 hours cooking the lamb should be soft and totally tender. Gently lift the meat from its tray, wrap it tightly in foil and leave to rest for at least 20 minutes.

While the lamb is resting, return the remaining 'mop' sauce to a saucepan and bring to the boil over a high heat. Boil vigorously until the sauce has reduced and is syrupy and just coats the back of a spoon. Turn the heat to low, finely chop the mint leaves and add them to the sauce. Add the butter and whisk into the sauce so it goes glossy.

When ready to serve, cut slices of the lamb away from the bone and arrange on a serving plate. Pour the reduced 'mop' sauce over the meat, making sure every piece is coated. Serve with our Perfect Pickled Potato Salad (see page 92) and Pickled Slaw (see page 95)

Pickle-brine chicken curry
with bread and butter raita

The jumping-off point for this recipe was a traditional vindaloo curry, which itself was derived from the Portuguese stew in which meat is tenderized in a heavily spiced, vinegar-based marinade before being cooked. We saw that and thought: 'pickle brine is basically heavily spiced vinegar, why not try using that instead?'

PICKLE-BRINE CHICKEN CURRY

500 g/1 lb. 2 oz. boneless chicken thighs, each cut into 3–4 large pieces

4 tablespoons Bread and Butter Spice Mix (see page 58)

1 teaspoon salt

250 ml/1 cup pickle brine (we use Bread and Butter Pickles brine, see page 58, but use whatever brine you have. If you don't have enough brine to hand, let down whatever you do have with equal parts water and vinegar)

1 tablespoon vegetable oil

2 large white onions, very finely sliced

a thumb-sized piece of fresh ginger, peeled and finely sliced

4 garlic cloves, thinly sliced

2 green chillies/chiles, finely sliced

2 red chillies/chiles, finely sliced

1 teaspoon ground turmeric

2 tablespoons tamarind paste

4 large tomatoes, roughly chopped

3 curry leaves (or more if you prefer)

basmati rice, to serve

BREAD AND BUTTER RAITA

1/2 large cucumber, grated

4 teaspoons salt

75 g/2³/4 oz. Bread and Butter Pickles (see page 58), brine drained and reserved, and pickles finely chopped

150 g/5¹/2 oz. full-fat yogurt

about 10 fresh mint leaves, very finely chopped

Serves 4

Place the chicken thighs in a bowl, add half the spice mix and the salt and toss to make sure the chicken is well coated. Add 100 ml/scant 1/2 cup of the pickle brine and massage to ensure the brine penetrates the chicken. Cover the bowl and leave in the fridge for at least one hour and up to 4 hours.

Meanwhile, heat the oil in a large, heavy-based saucepan over a medium heat. Add the onions and cook for about 20 minutes until they are very soft and starting to colour (turn the heat down if the onions are browning too quickly).

When the onions are very soft and a lovely golden colour, add the remaining spice mix, along with the ginger, garlic and chillies. Fry everything gently for another 5 minutes before adding the turmeric, tamarind and tomatoes. Give the mixture a stir so everything is well distributed. Turn up the heat and fry until the spices have released their flavour and the tomatoes are starting to collapse. At this point, pour in the remaining pickle brine and add the curry leaves, then bring the curry to a simmer. Cook for 30 minutes over a moderate heat, uncovered, until the sauce has thickened and is smelling incredible. Remove from the heat, allow to cool slightly before removing the curry leaves and blitzing to a smooth sauce with either a handheld stick/immersion blender in the pan itself or in a blender if you have one. If you don't possess either, the curry is still delicious (and probably slightly more authentic to its roots) left unblended, but we prefer the smooth curry sauce of Anglo-Indian restaurants. Return the curry sauce to a clean saucepan.

Take the chicken out of the brine. Let it drain slightly before adding to the sauce and returning the pan to the heat. Bring back to a gentle simmer and cook uncovered for 25–30 minutes until the chicken is cooked through and the sauce is thick and rich.

While the curry is cooking, make the raita. Mix the cucumber and salt in a bowl, leave for 10 minutes, then drain away any liquid that has been released. Stir in the pickles along with a tablespoon of brine. Add the yogurt and stir again to combine. Store in the fridge until you're ready to serve the curry. Just before serving, stir through the chopped mint.

When ready to eat, adjust the seasoning of the curry and add a little more pickle brine if the sauce is thick. Serve with rice and a big dollop of the raita.

Shedletskys salt beef with boiled potatoes

There always seems to be a bit of confusion over the actual differences between salt beef, pastrami and corned beef. Each one uses brisket and all have been staples of deli sandwiches for years. For the home cook, salt beef is by far the easiest of these preparations to achieve. It forgoes some of the complex smoky aromas of the best pastrami, but still achieves incredibly flavourful and tender results. The wet cure is forgiving and the cooking method is hard to mess up, so there aren't too many excuses not to have a go. This recipe does takes 5 days to cure, so do plan ahead.

a small beef brisket
joint (800 g–1.2 kg/
1 lb. 9 oz.–2¾ lb.)

BRINE (if curing the
beef yourself)

300 g/10½ oz. salt
(285 g/10 oz. if using
Prague Powder
Number One)

100 g/½ cup brown
sugar

100 g/½ cup white
sugar

3 dried bay leaves

10 whole cloves

½ tablespoon yellow
mustard seeds

½ tablespoon black
mustard seeds

½ tablespoon fennel
seeds

1 teaspoon dill seeds

½ teaspoon celery
seeds

1 teaspoon ground
turmeric

15 g/1 tablespoon
Prague Powder
Number One (also
sometimes called
Instacure #1)
(optional: using
it gives the meat
it's pink hue but
omitting it won't
affect the taste)

TO COOK
THE BRISKET

350 ml/1½ cups pickle
brine

500 ml/2 cups chicken
stock

½ teaspoon black
mustard seeds

½ teaspoon yellow
mustard seeds

2 whole cloves

½ teaspoon black
peppercorns

½ teaspoon ground
turmeric

1 teaspoon coriander
seeds

1 large carrot, peeled
and chopped

1 onion, peeled and
sliced into wedges

1 leek, rinsed of grit
and chopped

TO SERVE

boiled potatoes tossed
in butter and a few
herbs

boiled carrots

mustard, horseradish
sauce or chrain

**Serves 4
(or makes enough for
8 large sandwiches)**

Make a brine by dissolving the salt and both sugars in 2 litres/quarts water in a large saucepan over a medium heat. Add the bay leaves and all of the spices and continue to heat until the salt and sugar have completely dissolved. Remove from the heat and stir in the Prague Powder Number One, if using. Let the brine cool completely. Put the brisket joint in a large plastic or glass container with a lid and pour over the brine so the beef is completely submerged. Cover and store in the fridge for 5 days until the beef is cured.

After 5 days, remove the beef from the brine and rinse under cold running water. Discard the brine and clean the container. Return the beef to the container and cover in cold water. Leave to soak for a few hours, changing the water every hour to remove some of the saltiness. Once the beef has soaked for a few hours, preheat the oven to 160°C/140°C fan/325°F/Gas 3.

Add the pickle brine and stock to a small saucepan and bring to the boil. Add both mustard seeds, cloves, peppercorns, turmeric and coriander seeds and give everything a stir. In a deep casserole dish/ Dutch oven with a lid, add the carrot, onion and leek, then sit the beef on the vegetables. Pour the stock over the meat so it is almost completely covered. Immediately cover the dish with a double layer of foil and pop on the lid. Cook in the oven for 2–3 hours until the meat is very tender and wobbly but just holds its shape. Remove from the oven and leave to cool slightly in the brine before slicing and serving with boiled potatoes and carrots. Pour a little of the cooking liquid over the beef when you do this and consider serving mustard, horseradish or chrain on the side.

NOTE

Alternatively, let the salt beef cool in the brine, then use for sandwiches. The brine itself is also great for cooking beans or using as a base for soups. Just remember to check its saltiness before adding seasoning.

Pickled vegetable shawarma

Okay, so we know that this recipe is a bit of a faff. It has multiple stages and asks you to cook, press and chill things in an irritatingly 'cheffy' way, but the results really are worth the effort.

There's something fun about crafting a dish that really does look like one of those 'elephant leg' kebabs/kabobs, but rather than being made from dubious mystery meat, it's packed with lightly pickled vegetables. So if you ever find yourself with a cupboard full of root vegetables that need using up and a free afternoon to fill, it's well worth giving this recipe a go.

SHAWARMA

1 kg/2¼ lb. mixed root vegetables and squash (such as celeriac, butternut squash, swede, sweet potato), cut into very thin slices (using a mandolin if you have one)

500 g/2 cups white vinegar

1 tablespoon coriander seeds

1 tablespoon cumin seeds

½ tablespoon black peppercorns

½ teaspoon cloves

½ teaspoon dried chilli/hot red pepper flakes

½ tablespoon smoked paprika

½ tablespoon ground turmeric

½ tablespoon ground ginger

125 g/½ cup/1⅛ sticks butter

pinch of salt

2 tablespoons Hawaij spice mix (or mild curry powder)

TO ASSEMBLE

pitta breads, warmed or toasted

Instant Pickled Tomato and Cucumber Salad (see page 53)

Pink Pickled Turnips (see page 49)

Pickle-Brine Tahini Dip (see page 72)

hot sauce (see Note on page 71)

yogurt or labneh

16 x 24-cm/6 x 9½-inch deep baking dish lined with baking paper

Serves 6

Place the sliced veg in a plastic container large enough to accommodate them all. Bring the vinegar and 500 ml/2 cups water to the boil and add the coriander seeds, cumin seeds, peppercorns, cloves, chilli flakes, smoked paprika, turmeric and ginger. Stir to make sure anything soluble has dissolved. Pour the brine directly over the vegetables. Immediately cover with cling film/plastic wrap and set aside to pickle. After 2 hours, drain the vegetables and set aside.

Melt the butter in a small saucepan over a gentle heat with a pinch of salt. Stir through the Hawaij spice mix and remove from the heat. Preheat the oven to 180°C/160°C fan/350°F/Gas 4.

Start layering the vegetables in the prepared baking dish, brushing each layer with a generous amount of the spiced butter. Continue to add the vegetables and butter in layers, making sure the different veg are evenly distributed. Finish with a final spread of spiced butter. Wrap the whole dish in foil and press down with something heavy that is safe to go in the oven (we used our cast-iron sandwich press). Roast in the oven for 90 minutes or until a skewer goes through with only a tiny bit of resistance. Remove from the oven and leave to cool completely (still being pressed). Chill in the fridge for 4 hours. When completely cool, carefully remove the pressed vegetables from the pan.

You now have a couple of options. You can cut fingers from the now solid vegetables and crisp them up in a hot pan with just a little bit of oil. Alternatively, use a 10-cm/4-inch cookie cutter to cut out disks and stack them on top of each other. Wrap the tower tightly in foil and push one or two kebab skewers through the middle. Chill again while you heat the oven grill/broiler on high. When hot, unwrap the tower and carefully lay it over a bread tin/loaf pan. Place under the hot grill and cook (turning every 5 minutes) until the whole kebab is charred in places and piping hot throughout. Remove and slice into thin strips.

Assemble the pitta, salad, pickles and sauces on a plate along with a pile of the grilled vegetables so people can build their own stuffed pitta pockets.

Pickle panzanella salad

This salad is wonderful when you use beautiful, late summer fresh tomatoes. But the beauty of the quick pickle process we use at the start of this salad is that it really does extract the maximum tastiness from even the dullest supermarket tomatoes. As such, it's a fantastic example of how even the quickest pickle really amps up the flavour of dull ingredients. It's also a good way of using up those last pieces of stale bread so often leftover at the end of a loaf.

1 kg/2¼ lb. mixed tomatoes

1 tablespoon salt

1 teaspoon white sugar

1 tablespoon Italian Herb Mix (store-bought, or see page 37)

3 thick slices of stale bread (sourdough or ciabatta work well here, but any bread will do as long as it's not a pappy, white sliced loaf)

4 tablespoons brine from the Giardiniera pickles (see below)

4 tablespoons olive oil, plus a drizzle to serve

1 tablespoon red wine vinegar

1 tablespoon capers, drained

4 canned anchovy fillets in oil (optional)

1 cucumber

4 tablespoons Vaguely Italian Vegetable Giardiniera pickles (see page 37), drained, brine reserved

a handful of fresh basil

salt and freshly ground black pepper

Serves 4 as a side salad

Chop the tomatoes in a way that will look pleasing in a salad later: cut smaller ones in half and slice or quarter the larger ones. Place in a large bowl and cover with the salt, sugar and ½ tablespoon of the herb mix. Toss well, cover and set aside for 30 minutes.

While the tomatoes are curing, attend to your bread. Cut each slice into nice chunks – try to make them about the same size as the pieces of tomatoes you just prepared, but don't overly worry if some pieces are larger or small.

Assess how stale the bread is. If it's already hard, place straight into a small bowl. If it's still a little soft, pop it in a hot oven (preheated to 180°C/160°C fan/350°F/ Gas 4) for 10 minutes to dry it out before adding to the bowl. Once the bread is in the bowl, add 2 tablespoons of the pickle brine and toss so the bread can absorb the liquid.

After 30 minutes, drain the juice that has leeched from the tomatoes into a small bowl. Mix with the olive oil, remaining pickle brine and red wine vinegar and whisk. Roughly chop the capers and anchovies (if using) and add to the dressing. Taste and season with black pepper and a little salt if you think it's needed (it will be salty from the capers and anchovies).

Now it's time to assemble the salad. Cut the cucumber in half lengthways. Deseed it using a teaspoon and chop into 0.5-cm/¼-inch half moons. Take a pretty bowl that's large enough to accommodate the salad, add the tomatoes, cucumber, pickled vegetables and chunks of bread. Toss them all together with the remaining herb mix before pouring over the dressing. Toss again to make sure everything is well coated and set aside for 15 minutes to let everything soak up the flavours.

Just before serving, add the torn basil leaves and an extra drizzle of olive oil.

Pickled beetroot tart with goat's cheese

If you have a food processor, making shortcrust pastry is a simple process. And the results are far nicer than shop-bought. Plus, when you make your own pastry, you can play around with the flavours and sorts of flour you use, like using rye flour and caraway seeds to complement the pickled beetroot in this recipe.

1 teaspoon olive or vegetable oil

3 large red onions, finely sliced

100 ml/scant ½ cup balsamic vinegar

100 ml/scant ½ cup beetroot pickle brine

200 g/7 oz. ricotta

75 g/2¾ oz. sharp hard goat's cheese, plus extra to finish

2 teaspoons chopped fresh thyme

75 g/2¾ oz. soft goat's cheese log

250 g/9 oz. Borscht-style Pickled Beetroot (see page 46), cut into small cubes

1 egg

salt and freshly ground black pepper

PASTRY

200 g/1½ cups plain/all-purpose flour, plus extra for dusting

150 g/5½ oz. rye flour

225 g/1 cup/2 sticks cold butter, cut into small cubes

1 tablespoon caraway seeds

pinch of salt

**Makes 1 large tart –
enough to feed 8 at a picnic
or as an appetizer**

First, make the pastry. Add both flours to the bowl of a food processor and pulse to mix the flour thoroughly. Add the cold butter to the flour along with a pinch of salt and the caraway seeds. Pulse again until the mixture resembles fine breadcrumbs. Add 6 tablespoons very cold water and pulse again. Continue to pulse until the mixture comes together into a ball. Add an additional tablespoon of water, if needed, but be patient and try to get there without. Turn the pastry out onto a lightly floured surface. Knead briefly and wrap in cling film/plastic wrap. Refrigerate the pastry for at least 2 hours while you make the filling.

Heat the oil in a large saucepan over a medium heat. Add the onions and adjust the heat so they fry gently until caramelized and gooey (this should take around 30 minutes). Keep an eye on them and stir occasionally to ensure even cooking. When the onions look sweet and delicious, turn up the heat, add a pinch of salt, the balsamic vinegar and pickle brine. Scrape the pan to pick up any of the tasty cooked bits, allow the liquid to bubble merrily until it's sticky and delicious, then remove from the heat. Allow the onion mix to cool until needed.

Meanwhile, add the ricotta to another bowl. Grate the hard goat's cheese into the ricotta and whisk to combine. Add half the thyme leaves and season with lots of cracked black pepper. Whisk again and set aside.

Once the pastry has chilled for at least 2 hours, and roll it out on a well floured surface to a large rectangle that is an even 3 mm/⅛ inch thick.

Preheat the oven to 200°C/180°C fan/400°F/Gas 6 and line a large flat baking sheet with baking parchment.

Cut the pastry into a 30-cm/12-inch disk and carefully lift onto the baking sheet. Leaving a clear border around the edge, spread the onion mixture evenly across the pastry. Next, add spoonfuls of the ricotta mixture and small slices of the soft goat's cheese. Arrange the beetroot over the cheese. Carefully fold inwards and crimp the lip of pastry to form a ridged edge. Whisk the egg and brush across the pastry. Scatter the remaining thyme leaves over the top of the tart. Bake in the oven for 40 minutes until the pastry is a deep, even brown. If the pastry still looks pale after 40 minutes, give it an extra 10 minutes, but take it out of the oven as soon as it looks like it might be catching.

Remove from the oven and top with an extra grating of hard goat's cheese. Serve immediately while warm or serve at room temperature with a crisp green salad.

Pickle-cooked chips with pickle gravy and fried cheese

This is perhaps our most rogue use of pickle brine in this book, but there *is* method to the idea! After all, Heston Blumenthal's famous triple-cooked chips/fries recipe calls for a splash of vinegar in the water used to cook the potatoes to help them hold their shape and stay fluffy. The brine also adds flavour and means you don't have to make your chips soggy by dowsing them in vinegar after frying.

CHIPS

4 large Maris Piper potatoes, peeled and cut into chips

300 ml/1¼ cups Bread and Butter Pickles brine (see page 58) – or another type of pickle brine

salt

vegetable oil, for frying

PICKLE GRAVY

3 tablespoons unsalted butter

1 tablespoon plain/all-purpose flour

2 teaspoons tomato purée/paste

150 ml/²⁄₃ cup pickle brine

250 ml/1 cup stock (instant chicken or vegetable is fine)

1 tablespoon soy sauce

2 tablespoons capers, drained and roughly chopped

100 g/3½ oz. Bread and Butter Pickles (see page 58), drained and roughly chopped

freshly ground black pepper

TO SERVE

250 g/9 oz. halloumi, cut into 1-cm/½-inch cubes

Serves 2 as a side dish or enough chips for 3–4 people

NOTE
Poutine in Canada usually uses cheese curds but these are hard to track down, so we use halloumi as it has a similar squeaky nature and can be happily deep fried.

Place the chipped potatoes in a large bowl and rinse in cold running water until the water runs clear and all the excess starch has been removed. Transfer the chips to a large saucepan and cover with the pickle brine and 700 ml/2¾ cups water. Add a pinch of salt. Bring to the boil and cook at a rolling boil for about 15 minutes until they are very soft but not yet collapsing. Carefully drain the chips and let them cool. Once cool, lay the chips on a rack and place in the fridge uncovered for at least 3 hours to dry out completely.

When ready to cook, fill a deep-fat fryer to the fill line with oil and heat to 140°C/285°F. Once the oil is hot enough, remove the chips from the fridge. Working in batches, add half to the frying basket (avoid overcrowding the fryer, so only add a third of the chips, depending on the fryer's capacity). Fry the chips for 4 minutes, remove and allow to drain on a baking sheet lined with paper towels. You don't want the chips to colour too much: they should just take on a light golden colour. Once all the chips have had their first fry, either allow them to cool and chill again in the fridge for another 3 hours before the final fry or move straight on to their final fry. (Chilling them a second time yields slightly fluffier results.)

Between the first and second fry is the perfect time to make the pickle gravy. To do this, melt the butter in a small saucepan over a medium heat. When melted, stir in the flour and cook to make a light roux. Add the tomato purée and cook for a few minutes. Add the pickle brine and stir to combine; the mixture should come together and then thicken. Continue to stir until you have a thick, smooth mixture. Stir in the stock and cook again until you have a gravy-like consistency. Add more stock if it's a little thick. Add the soy sauce and season with black pepper. Stir the capers and pickles through the gravy. Keep warm while you finish the chips.

When ready for the final fry, first preheat the oven to 120°C/100°C fan/340°F/Gas ¼, then heat the oil in the fryer to 190°C/375°F. Again working in batches to avoid overcrowding, fry the chips for 90 seconds or until golden brown. Drain again on paper towels and keep warm in the oven on a baking sheet.

Drop the halloumi cubes into the deep-fat fryer. Cook for a couple of minutes until golden brown and then remove and allow to drain.

To assemble, salt the chips and add to a plate. Top with deep-fried halloumi and then liberally smother everything with the pickle gravy.

Perfect pickle potato salad

All too often potato salads are a gloopy affair of bland potatoes bound with too much mayonnaise. It's a shame because done well, this is a wonderful side dish that complements almost anything cooked on the grill, as well as being our default option to bring to picnics and outdoor events in the summer.

Our German friend Claire introduced us to the more northern European style of potato salads, where the tubers are dressed in a vinaigrette rather than covered in mayonnaise. We still use mayo but dial it back and add a pickle-brine-charged dressing before absolutely loading the mixture with more pickles and other briney delights to make something that's fresh yet comforting at the same time.

500 g/1 lb. 2 oz. waxy potatoes

1 teaspoon salt

1 teaspoon Dijon mustard

2 tablespoons pickle brine

2 tablespoons vegetable oil

1 teaspoon hot sauce
(see Note on page 71)

2 tablespoons good-quality
mayonnaise

50-g/1¾-oz. can of anchovy fillets
in oil

1 tablespoon good-quality capers
(washed if stored in salt, drained
if stored in brine)

1 tablespoon Bread and Butter
Pickles (see page 58)

1 tablespoon additional pickles
(use whatever other pickles you
have on hand here – we used
the Dr. Brown's Pickled Celery
from page 45, but use whatever
you fancy)

1 tablespoon snipped fresh chives

1 tablespoon chopped fresh dill

2 spring onions/scallions, finely
chopped

1 teaspoon Pickled Mustard Seeds
(see page 38, optional)

salt and freshly ground black pepper

Serves 4 as a side

Peel the potatoes and chop any larger ones into 3-cm/1¼-inch pieces. You're aiming for even-sized potato pieces that will work in the salad, so chop accordingly.

Fill a saucepan with water and salt generously. Add the potatoes and bring to the boil over a medium heat. Cook for about 12–15 minutes until the potatoes are tender but not yet starting to break apart.

Meanwhile, in a large bowl, combine the salt with the mustard, pickle brine and vegetable oil and whisk to make a dressing. Set aside

When the potatoes are cooked, drain and immediately add the warm potatoes to the bowl with the dressing. Toss gently to coat the potatoes, cover and leave them to cool in the dressing.

In a separate bowl, combine the hot sauce with the mayonnaise. Drain and chop the anchovies, capers and the two types of pickles. Add these to the mayonnaise mixture and stir to combine.

Add the herbs and spring onions to the mayo along with the pickled mustard seeds (if using).

When the potatoes are cool and have absorbed most of the pickle dressing, add all of the pickle-packed mayo and gently stir everything to combine. Taste and season with black pepper. It's probably salty enough at this point, but add more too, if you think it needs it.

Place in a pretty serving bowl (or suitable airtight container if this is heading to a picnic/BBQ). Scatter over some extra herbs and dot with a few more pickled mustard seeds before serving.

Pickle slaw

There's something inherently depressing about the typical coleslaw on offer at most barbecues. Bland cabbage in gloopy mayonnaise isn't doing anyone any favours. To us, it recalls burnt sausages, charred-yet-pink-in-the-middle chicken and bowls of supermarket own-brand crisps and dips.

To counteract the blandness, our slaw is quickly pickled and then dressed in a lighter-than-normal, yogurt-based dressing that brings much needed freshness to proceedings. We also pack our slaw with herbs and boost the flavour further with a hit of Curtido. The result? Something that is fresh enough to cut through the fattiest smoked meat to banish any memories of sheltering under a dripping gazebo eating a sad hot dog off a soggy paper plate while it pours with rain.

½ large white cabbage
 (about 600 g/1 lb. 5 oz.)

2 large carrots

2 sticks/ribs of celery

10 breakfast radishes

1 red onion

2 tablesoons salt

2 teaspoons white sugar

200 g/7 oz. Curtido (see page 57),
 drained

2 green apples

1 green (bell) pepper

2 tablespoons pickled jalapeños

selection of mixed fresh herbs
 (a mix of tarragon, dill, mint
 and parsley, for example)
 – roughly a bunch in total

4 tablespoons pickling brine from
 the Curtido (see above)

4 tablespoons olive oil

2 tablespoons white vinegar

1 tablespoon honey

250 g/1 cup Greek yogurt

salt and freshly ground black pepper

TO SERVE

best-quality olive oil

2 tablespoons mixed chopped fresh
 herbs, as before

**Makes enough for 8–10
people at a BBQ or picnic**

Cut the cabbage half in half again so you have quarters, then slice out the tough core and discard. Shred the cabbage into very thin slices and add to a large bowl. Peel the carrots and slice into thin matchsticks. Add to the bowl with the cabbage. Slice the radishes thinly and add to the bowl. Peel the onion, slice in half and cut into very thin half moons. Pop it into the bowl with the rest of the vegetables.

Add the salt and sugar to the bowl and stir through the vegetables until they are very well mixed in. Set aside for 30 minutes.

After 30 minutes, tip away most of the liquid that has pooled at the bottom of the bowl. Add the drained Curtido to the rest of the vegetables. Peel the apples and remove the cores, then slice into thin matchsticks. Thinly slice the pepper and pickled jalapeños and add both to the slaw. Pick the leaves from the herbs, finely shred them and stir through the slaw.

In a separate bowl, whisk together the Curtido pickling brine, olive oil, vinegar and honey.

When ready to serve, add the dressing to the slaw. Toss to coat all the ingredients. Finally, stir through the yogurt so every piece is lightly coated. Taste and adjust the seasoning with salt and a little cracked black pepper.

Arrange the slaw on a large serving platter or bowl and finish with a little extra olive oil and two more tablespoons of finely chopped herbs.

Some Sandwiches

Grilled cheese and pickle sandwich

It's funny how one recipe combines so many elements of the Shedletskys ethos in two pieces of bread and a filling. First, there's our love of the classics. In this case, the humble cheese and pickle sandwich. That collides with a desire to do things differently where possible. So instead of making just another toasted cheese sandwich, we've gone for something more interesting: a Shedletskys take on the croque. Finally, there's a bit of science at play, leveraging sodium citrate (see note) to help the cheese melt into the pickle brine without splitting or becoming greasy. When we bring it all together, you get something that is absolutely Shedletskys while still hopefully honouring the original.

4 slices of sourdough bread

2 tablespoons butter

3 tablespoons shop-bought sweet sandwich pickle

4 tablespoons pickled red onions

1 tablespoon French mustard

200 g/2 cups mixed grated Cheddar and Emmental cheese

PICKLE CHEESE SPREAD

100 ml/scant $^1/_2$ cup white wine

100 ml/scant $^1/_2$ cup pickle brine

15 g/1 tablespoon sodium citrate

$^1/_2$ tablespoon mustard powder

$^1/_2$ tablespoon white sugar

$^1/_4$ teaspoon garlic powder

$^1/_2$ teaspoon onion powder

100 g/1 cup grated Cheddar

100 g/1 cup grated Emmental

100 g/1 cup grated Gruyére

1 tablespoon any hot sauce (see Note on page 71)

1 tablespoon Henderson's Relish (or Worcestershire sauce if you must)

100 g/3$^1/_2$ oz. Bread and Butter Pickles (see page 58), chopped

Makes 2 sandwiches

A NOTE ON SODIUM CITRATE:
Sodium citrate is an acidity regulator that enables cheeses to melt without becoming greasy. It's safe to eat and you can buy it online.

To make the cheese spread, add the wine and pickle brine to a saucepan and warm over a medium heat. Add the sodium citrate, mustard powder and sugar and whisk to dissolve. As it starts to simmer, whisk in the garlic and onion powders. Turn the heat to low and add the different cheeses, 100 g/1 cup at a time. Keep the heat low and continue to whisk each addition of cheese until it's fully melted before adding the next batch. When all the cheese is completely melted and the mixture is smooth, turn off the heat and whisk in the hot sauce and Henderson's Relish. Fold the chopped pickles through the cheese. Let cool, whisking regularly so the spread does not form a skin. Once cool, scrape the spread into a tub and store in the fridge until needed.

To assemble the sandwiches, first turn the oven grill/broiler on high. Next, melt the butter in a pan. Lay all four slices of bread on a baking sheet and brush the upward side of each slice with melted butter. Grill/broil until golden brown. Turn two pieces of bread over and set the other two pieces aside for later. Divide the sweet sandwich spread between the two remaining pieces of bread, then top each with the pickled red onions. Cover this with the additional cheese and return the pan to the grill to melt the cheese.

Meanwhile, spread the untoasted sides of the other two pieces of bread with mustard. When the grilled cheese is melted, remove the pan from the grill. Add the reserved bread, with the toasted side facing upwards. Spread each sandwich with a thick layer of the pickle cheese spread, ensuring the whole top of the sandwich is well covered. Return to the grill one more time and cook until the cheese spread is bubbling and slightly charred in places. Remove from the grill and serve, perhaps with a salad to cut through the cheesiness.

NOTE
You'll have plenty of cheese spread left after making this recipe. Store in the fridge and use within a week. It can be used as a dip, in place of cheese on a burger, or to make mac & cheese by par-cooking a packet of macaroni, then tossing the warm and drained pasta with the cheese spread before baking in the oven.

Chicken mayo sandwich

We often make chicken mayo sandwiches to use up the last scraps of a roast chicken before the carcass becomes stock. The sheer number of punchy pickles we add to the mixture not only means you can get several sandwiches from not a lot of chicken, but it really peps up meat that was cooked a few days before.

There are times when the urge for a chicken sandwich hits and you don't have a roast bird to hand. This is the recipe for those moments, using a couple of legs as they cook more quickly than a whole bird (and even we think cooking a whole chicken to make sandwiches at home might be taking things too far).

On the pickles used here... it is very much just a suggestion. We generally use whatever pickles we have on hand. Use whatever is available, but just make sure you have 2 tablespoons to go into your mixture so it really is 'pickle-packed'.

8 thickly cut, slices of good-quality white bread

good-quality salted butter, softened to room temperature

6 fresh radishes, thinly sliced

salad leaves

CHICKEN MAYO MIX

2 chicken legs

1 lemon

1 garlic clove

2¼ tablespoons pickle brine

1 tablespoon olive or vegetable oil

2 tablespoons good-quality mayonnaise

1 tablespoon natural/plain yogurt

1 tablespoon Bread and Butter Pickles (see page 58), roughly chopped

½ tablespoon Pickled Green Tomatoes (see page 61), chopped

½ tablespoon Dr. Brown's Pickled Celery (see page 45), chopped

1 tablespoon chopped fresh tarragon

1 tablespoon chopped fresh dill

1 tablespoon chopped fresh parsley

salt and freshly ground black pepper

Makes enough for 4 generous sandwiches

Preheat the oven to 180°C/160°C fan/350°F/Gas 4.

Place the chicken legs in a small roasting pan. Season with salt and pepper. Halve the lemon and squeeze the juice over the chicken. Lightly crush the garlic clove and add to the roasting pan, along with the lemon halves.

In a small bowl, mix together 2 tablespoons of the brine and the oil, then drizzle over the chicken.

Roast the chicken in the preheated oven for 35 minutes until the meat is cooked through and the skin is golden brown. Remove from the oven and leave to cool.

When cool, carefully pick the cooked meat from the chicken legs along with the chicken skin. Chop all the meat into bite-sized chunks and add to a bowl. Slice the skin into strips and reserve for later.

Take the roasted garlic clove and mash it. Add this to the bowl with the meat. Drizzle over a tablespoon of the roasting juices. Add the mayonnaise and yogurt and stir to combine. Add the chopped pickles and herbs and stir through. Finally, add the remaining pickle brine and mix. Taste and adjust the seasoning with salt and pepper.

To assemble the sandwiches, butter the slices of bread. Add a layer of salad leaves to half the buttered bread slices. Top with the chicken mixture, then sliced radish and chicken skin. Finally, close the sandwiches, press down gently, cut into halves and enjoy.

Pickled egg salad sando

Nat is an absolute egg salad queen. She gets requests from members of her shul (synagogue) to make sure one is always included whenever she organizes kiddush. And there's never been a single instance when any of her delicious mixture has made it back home from synagogue for me to enjoy.

It's all part of her on-going egg love affair. It's a passion that has seen her peeling hundreds of boiled eggs so we could serve devilled eggs at a pop-up. Plus it means she is the only person I know who actively has 'an egg guy'.

This sandwich takes Nat's essential egg salad recipe and brings an added pickle element into play by dropping whole pickled eggs into the equation. Construction owes something to the Japanese Tamago Sandos *that crop up on social media every few years, while the pickle-heavy mix is very much a Shedletskys favourite.*

8 thickly cut slices of good-quality white bread (ideally Japanese milk bread but any good white loaf will work), crusts removed

rocket/arugula

EGG MAYO

6 fresh (ideally free-range) eggs (4 are for the egg mayo and 2 are for pickling whole)

150 ml/⅔ cup Bread and Butter Pickles brine (see page 58)

4 tablespoons best-quality mayonnaise

2 tablespoons English mustard

2 teaspoons caper brine

1 tablespoon capers, roughly chopped

1 tablespoon pickles of your choice, roughly chopped (Bread and Butter Pickles on page 58, Dr. Brown's Pickled Celery on page 45 or Vaguely Italian Vegetable Giardiniera pickles on page 37 all work well)

1 tablespoon chopped fresh herbs (chives, dill, tarragon, cress, etc.)

Makes enough for 4 sandwiches

First, make the egg mayo filling. Take a saucepan large enough to accommodate all the eggs and with a lid, add the eggs to the pan and cover them with cold water. Place the pan on the hob/stovetop and bring to the boil, uncovered, over a medium-high heat. The moment the water starts to boil, bring the heat right down so the water is just shimmering. Place the lid on and start your timer.

After 6 minutes, remove 2 of the eggs and cool under cold running water. After another 2 minutes have passed (so 8 minutes in total), remove the other 4 eggs and cool under cold running water. Make sure you remember which eggs are which at this point!

Peel the 6-minute eggs. Fill a small bowl or pot with the pickle brine and drop these two peeled eggs into the brine. Use a piece of paper towel to keep the eggs submerged in the brine for at least an hour, but no more than 4 hours.

While the eggs are curing, peel the 8-minute eggs and add to a bowl. Use a potato ricer or a fork to mash the eggs into the bowl. Add the mayonnaise, mustard and caper brine and stir to combine. Add the capers, pickles and herbs and stir through the mixture. Season with salt and pepper.

To assemble the sandwiches, place 4 slices of bread on a chopping board and cover each with an even amount of the egg mayo filling.

Remove the pickled eggs from the brine and cut each in half lengthways. Place one half in the centre of each sandwich and press lightly down so they are cradled by the egg mayo around them.

Top with a generous handful of rocket and close the sandwiches with the remaining bread. Slice each sandwich in half, aiming to bisect each of the pickled egg halves.

The Shedletskys Hot – a fried chicken
sandwich with pickles and hot sauce

The original version of this sandwich was created at Prince's Hot Chicken Shack in Nashville. The exact details of its genesis are cloaked in myth and speculation, but what is certain is that we tried this particular spicy sandwich when we visited Nashville and loved it. The crispy chicken. The abundant, almost offensively hot sauce. The single piece of cheap white bread soaking up everything. The pickles providing some much-needed cut-through. The perfect sandwich? It's certainly possible.

In the years since, we've made lots of different versions of this sandwich. Some used the more traditional fried chicken of the Deep South and some, like this version, took the essential elements but used a more European breaded chicken escalope. The advantage of this technique is that it makes the whole cooking process much quicker, so you can enjoy this great sandwich without unnecessary delays.

4 tablespoons hot sauce
  (see Note on page 71)
4 tablespoons pickle brine
2 tablespoons French's mustard
8 slices of cheap white bread,
  the pappier the better
  (or just use 4 slices and
  serve as open sandwiches)
mayonnaise
Bread and Butter Pickles
  (see page 58)
shredded iceberg lettuce

BREADED CHICKEN
4 chicken thighs, skinned
  and boned
4 tablespoons plain/
  all-purpose flour
2 tablespoons Dried Pickle Dust
  (see page 134, optional)
2 eggs
2 tablespoons pickle brine
6 tablespoons fine matzo meal
2 tablespoons vegetable oil
salt

**Makes enough for
4 generous sandwiches**

First, make the breaded chicken. Place one of the chicken pieces between two sheets of baking parchment and beat with a rolling pin until very thin (about 5 mm/ 1/8 inch thick all over). Repeat with the rest of the chicken.

Take three large lipped plates. Add the flour and pickle dust (if using) to the first and season with salt. Break the eggs onto the second plate and whisk with the pickle brine. On the third plate, add the fine matzo meal. Working one piece at a time, coat the chicken first in seasoned flour (making sure it's completely covered), then into the egg on both sides, and finally into the matzo meal. Repeat until all the chicken is coated.

Preheat the oven to 140°C/120°C fan/300°F/Gas 2.

Heat the oil in a large non-stick frying pan/skillet that will accommodate two pieces of chicken at a time over a medium heat. When the oil shimmers, add the chicken and fry undisturbed for 3–4 minutes until golden brown. Adjust the heat if it looks like the coating is burning. Carefully turn the pieces over and fry on the other side until golden brown and cooked through. Drain on paper towels, then place the cooked chicken on a baking sheet and keep warm in the oven while you repeat for the rest of the chicken. Add an additional tablespoon of oil if you think the pan is looking a little dry.

While the final pieces of chicken are cooking, prepare the other elements of your sandwich. Add the hot sauce to a small bowl and mix with the pickle brine and mustard. Slather each piece of bread with mayonnaise, then add a piece of cooked chicken. Dust with additional pickle dust if you have any available and then drench with as much of the hot sauce mix as you can tolerate. Top with several slices of pickle, shredded lettuce and a second slice of mayo-spread bread to close the sandwich.

Pickle-loaded muffin-etta
(a tribute to the Wilensky's Special)

It's funny how many of our trips end up centered around sandwiches. We've made significant detours to try everything from a Nashville Hot Chicken Sandwich to the 'Instant Heart Attack' at Second Avenue Deli in New York.

Two sandwiches really stand out. The famous meat-and-cheese-fest that is the Muffuletta from Central Grocery in New Orleans and the less well known Wilensky's Special from Wilensky's Light Lunch. This kosher-style lunch counter on Fairmount Avenue West in Montreal has been open since the 1930s and is (last time we visited) still run by relations of the original owner. They serve what is essentially a very simple grilled bologna sandwich on an English muffin. And it's delicious.

Here, we've taken some of the elements of the Wilensky's Special and others from the Muffuletta to create a tribute to two of the best sandwiches we've ever eaten.

4 English muffins

1 tablespoon olive oil, plus extra for drizzling

1 ripe tomato

1/2 teaspoon Italian Herb Mix (shop-bought or make your own, see page 37)

75 g/2³/4 oz. stoned/pitted green olives

100 g/3¹/2 oz. Borscht-Style Pickled Beetroot (see page 46)

8 slices of Emmental cheese

100 g/3¹/2 oz. Vaguely Italian Vegetable Giardiniera pickles (see page 37)

1 small Blooms Salami Chub (or other soft beef salami)

4 teaspoons capers, drained, rinsed and roughly chopped

2 tablespoons chopped fresh parsley

salt and freshly ground black pepper

Makes 4 sandwiches

Slice the muffins in half across the middle and drizzle with olive oil. Slice the tomato and add two slices to four of the muffin halves. Sprinkle the tomato slices with the herb mix and a little salt. Add a quarter of the green olives and a quarter of the beetroot to each. Lay 2 slices of cheese over each sandwich, then top with the Giardiniera.

Slice the salami into 5-mm/¹/8-inch rounds. Cut tiny nicks around the edges of each piece to prevent them curling up. Heat a large frying pan/skillet and add the slices. Use a press to keep them flat while you fry them. Cook over a medium heat until the salami is starting to crisp up – a matter of a couple of minutes – and then turn each piece and cook for a further 5 minutes until crispy. Remove from the heat and distribute across the sandwiches.

Scatter the sandwiches with chopped capers and parsley, then season with salt and pepper and drizzle with a little more olive oil.

Top with the other halves of the muffins, then use a baking sheet to press down the sandwiches. Sit a few heavy cookbooks on top to press the sandwiches. Leave for 30–60 minutes after which time the sandwiches have compacted and the flavours have melded together.

Meatball sub with pickled tomato sauce

Most times when we make meatball sandwiches, we're using up leftovers from a dish of spaghetti and meatballs. And this recipe works perfectly well if you want to do that. The only issue is if you're a greedy guts like us, you'll eat too many meatballs the night before and there won't be enough for a decent sandwich. Our solution? Double the quantities here and make a huge batch of meatballs and sauce. That way you can gorge without any worries about meagre sandwiches tomorrow.

MEATBALLS

50 g/1³⁄₄ oz. stale bread
50 ml/3¹⁄₂ tablespoons pickle brine
1 tablespoon tomato ketchup
1 tablespoon French's mustard
500 g/1 lb. 2 oz. minced/ground beef
100 g/¹⁄₂ cup Vaguely Italian Vegetable Giardiniera pickles (see page 37)
75 g/2¹⁄₂ oz. Parmesan cheese, grated
¹⁄₂ tablespoon salt
1 tablespoon chopped fresh thyme
1 tablespoon Italian Herb Mix (see page 37 or shop-bought)

SAUCE

1 tablespoon olive oil
2 garlic cloves, thinly sliced
2 pickled tomatoes, chopped
¹⁄₄ pickled chilli/chile, chopped
100 ml/scant ¹⁄₂ cup pickle brine
400-g/14-oz. can chopped tomatoes
100 g/3¹⁄₂ oz. Vaguely Italian Vegetable Giardiniera pickles (see page 37)
2 tablespoons Italian Herb Mix (see page 37 or shop-bought)
1 tablespoon white sugar
freshly ground black pepper

FOR THE SANDWICHES

soft white submarine rolls
1 Pickled Green Tomato (see page 61), chopped
150 g/5¹⁄₂ oz. mozzarella cheese
French's mustard

Makes 4 sandwiches
or dinner for 2 with enough
leftover for 2 sandwiches

First, rip the stale bread into chunks and put them in a large bowl. Pour the pickle brine over the bread and let it soak for 10 minutes. Once soft, mash the bread into a pickle-y paste. Add the ketchup and mustard, forming a (let's be honest) odd-looking mix. Add the beef, pickles (chopped if big), Parmesan, salt, thyme and herb mix to the bowl. Use your hands to gently mix it together, being careful not to overwork it (or you'll end up with tough meatballs).

Take about 50 g/1³⁄₄ oz. of the meatball mix and set it aside for the sauce. Shape the rest into golf ball-sized balls, keeping your hands slightly wet to help. Put them on a baking sheet and chill for 10–15 minutes to firm up.

Now, make the tomato sauce. Heat the olive oil in a saucepan over medium heat. Add the reserved meatball mix and cook until it starts to brown. Add the garlic and when it smells fragrant and is just turning brown, add the pickled tomatoes and chilli. Stir everything, scraping up any bits stuck to the pan. Cook this for a few minutes until the tomatoes start to break down. Then, add the remaining pickle brine and the chopped tomatoes from the can. Season with sugar and pepper, and simmer uncovered for 45 minutes. At this point, you can blend the sauce for a smooth finish, or leave it chunky.

Heat more olive oil in a non-stick frying pan/skillet. Add the meatballs and cook without moving them for 4 minutes per side, until browned all over. As they cook, bring the tomato sauce back to a simmer. Gently drop the meatballs into the sauce, so they're half covered. Cook for 15 minutes, until the meatballs are cooked through.

You can either serve the meatballs with spaghetti or make sandwiches. If you're using leftovers for sandwiches, reheat the sauce and meatballs before assembly.

To make the sandwiches, preheat the oven grill/broiler. Slice open the sub rolls and put them on a baking sheet. Put a few pickled tomatoes in the bottom of each roll. Add the meatballs to each roll, packing them enough so there's some in every bite. Cover with the tomato sauce, and scatter the mozzarella on top. Grill until the cheese has melted and the sauce is bubbling. Drizzle with mustard before serving.

Vegetarian pambazo sandwich
with potatoes, paprika and hot sauce

On a trip to Mexico, instead of spending time by the hotel pool, we set off for Mexico City's central food market. After several hours exploring the market, we found a cafe right at its heart. There, sitting on plastic chairs, we first tried a pambazo sandwich. We've since learned there are lots of versions of a pambazo, but the one we tried that day featured a deliciously soft roll that was dipped in sauce, then grilled. Here we've omitted the chorizo that was used, replacing it with crispy, pickle-cooked potatoes. The result is something that is both recognizably a pambazo but also owes something to the classic chip butty of British fish and chip shops.

4 large potatoes, peeled and cut into 1.5-cm/$^1/_2$-inch cubes

300 ml/1$^1/_4$ cups pickle brine

1 teaspoon salt, plus extra for seasoning the potatoes

2 tablespoons vegetable oil

$^1/_2$ teaspoon hot paprika

1 teaspoon smoked paprika

$^1/_2$ teaspoon vinegar powder (can be bought online)

200 g/$^3/_4$ cup/1$^3/_4$ sticks butter

100 ml/scant $^1/_2$ cup hot sauce (see Note on page 71)

2 large soft bread rolls

'Curtido' South American Pickled Cabbage (see page 57)

mayonnaise

Makes 2 large sandwiches

Place the potatoes in a colander/strainer and rinse under cold water until it runs clear. Drain and add the potatoes to a large saucepan. Cover with the pickle brine and 700 ml/2$^3/_4$ cups water. Add the 1 teaspoon of salt and bring to the boil over a high heat. Cook for 10–15 minutes until the potatoes are very soft but haven't collapsed completely. When the potatoes are cooked, remove from the heat and drain. Leave the potatoes to steam dry.

Meanwhile, preheat the oven to 200°C/180°C fan/400°F/Gas 6. Put a lipped baking sheet in the oven while it is heating so it gets hot too. Add the oil to the hot baking sheet and return to the oven to heat for 5 minutes.

Once the potatoes dry, return them to the pan they were cooked in and add both the paprikas and a pinch of salt to season. Toss vigorously in the pan until all the potatoes are well coated and their edges are slightly scuffed and craggy.

Carefully tip the potatoes onto the baking sheet and return to the oven to cook for 40 minutes, turning once after 25 minutes, until crispy. Remove from the oven and toss with another pinch of salt and the vinegar powder.

Just before the potatoes are due to come out of the oven, melt the butter in a small saucepan. Add the hot sauce and whisk to combine.

Heat a large frying pan/skillet over a medium heat and cut the bread rolls in half. Dunk the rolls in the melted butter/hot sauce combo, then toast them in the hot pan until both sides are starting to brown.

Remove the rolls from the pan and start to build the sandwiches. Start with a piece of the sauce-saturated bread roll. Top with potatoes, then a large handful of drained Curtido and a smear of mayo. Drizzle over a little more of the sauce and close the sandwich with a second piece of hot-sauce fried bread. Press down and serve immediately with the remaining sauce for dunking.

Chopped liver sandwich with pickled beetroot

I feel like chopped liver has a bit of an image problem. It's all in the name, really. Traditionally, kosher laws around cooking offal also meant that chopped liver ran the risk of being particularly grey and grainy. Again, adding to the dish's unappealing nature. But, and here's the thing, done right, chopped liver is just as delicious as the fanciest French pâté. The slow-cooked onions give it an added sweetness that the chicken fat that's used in most traditional recipes only enhances. The chopped egg adds richness and a nice textural contrast. Served in a soft roll, with plenty of mustard and a nice punchy pickle, there really is nothing better.

50 g/1³/₄ oz. smaltz (or oil, or butter)

2 large white onions (about 200 g/7 oz.), thinly sliced

400 g/14 oz. chicken liver, excess fat and sinews trimmed

125 ml/¹/₂ cup Bread and Butter Pickles brine (see page 58)

3 hard-boiled/cooked free-range eggs

salt and freshly ground black pepper

2 soft challah rolls (or similar)

100 g/3¹/₂ oz. Borscht-Style Pickled Beetroot (see page 46)

hot English mustard

Makes 2 rolls

A QUICK NOTE ON FAT

Most recipes for chicken liver pâté call for chicken schmaltz – the tasty yellow fat you get making stock from scratch or rendering down chicken skin. Obviously, if you happen to have this sitting in your fridge, use it. But if you don't, you can get really good results using a neutral oil (or butter providing you're not worried about the kosher rules around mixing meat and milk).

Heat a large frying pan/skillet over a medium heat and add your fat of choice. When it's hot enough, add the onions with a pinch of salt and cook gently for 15 minutes until the onions are soft and golden.

Remove the onions to a bowl from the pan, turn up the heat and add the liver. Cook over a high heat for 3 minutes until the edges of the livers are starting to brown. Flip the livers over and cook for a further 4 minutes on the other side. Cut one of the larger pieces in half. Are they cooked through without a trace of pink? If yes, then they're ready. If not, cook for a minute longer.

Once cooked, remove the livers from the pan and add to the bowl with the onions. Return the pan to the heat and add the pickle brine. Leave to bubble and reduce, scraping the pan with a wooden spoon to pick up any tasty bits that have stuck to the bottom during the cooking process. When you've got a nice thick syrup, add to the bowl with the liver and onions and stir to combine.

Transfer the liver, onions and deglazed pan juices to the bowl of a food processor along with two of the boiled eggs. Pulse until coarsely chopped but be careful not to reduce the mixture to a fine pâté. Season to taste with salt and plenty of black pepper. Alternatively, chop all the ingredients by hand.

Once chopped, remove from the food processor and add to a bowl. Grate the remaining hard-boiled egg over the top of the mixture. This is now ready to serve, either in a sandwich or however else you prefer (we've been known to just eat it with a spoon the moment it's made). You will only need about half the chopped liver mixture for the rolls, unless you are making for more people. Anything left will keep in the fridge for 3–4 days.

To assemble the sandwiches, split the rolls in half. Liberally smear the both sides of the rolls with hot mustard. On the bottom of each roll, add the chopped liver (it should be thick enough for you to see your teeth marks when you bite into it), top with pickled beetroot and add the mustard-adorned top of the roll. Press down lightly so the pickle brine merges with the pâté and serve.

Reuben flatbread with pastrami, pickles, cheese and Russian dressing

Oh, what a combination. Soft, fatty salt beef. Oozy cheese. Punchy pickled bits. All united by a piquant, briney dressing. Without a doubt, this is another entrant in our 'top sandwiches of the world' list. And the good thing is, once you have a piece of salt beef cooked from the recipe on page 83, the sandwich itself is relatively easy to put together, especially if you have a jar of sauerkraut in the fridge (and if you don't, making our 'quick kraut' cabbage below means you can have something approximating the ferment in just an hour).

At Katz Deli, the Reubens are stacked so high, the top piece of bread often falls off or collapses. To mitigate this sandwich construction disaster, we've simply taken it out of the equation and made an open flatbread.

2 large flatbreads (preferably made using our pickle-brine dough on pages 137–8, or any other good-quality flatbread)

500 g/1 lb. 2 oz. cooked salt beef (see page 83)

6 slices of Emmental cheese

Bread and Butter Pickles (see page 58)

QUICK KRAUT

½ large white cabbage

1 tablespoon olive oil

2 teaspoons caraway seeds

250 ml/1 cup white wine

2 teaspoons salt

freshly ground black pepper

50 ml/3½ tablespoons white wine vinegar

20 g/1½ tablespoons butter

REUBEN DRESSING

100 g/½ cup mayonnaise

35 g/2 tablespoons tomato ketchup

1 tablespoon horseradish sauce

1 tablespoon wholegrain mustard

2 tablespoons pickle brine

Makes 2 large flatbreads, enough for 4 people

Start by making the quick kraut. Halve the cabbage and remove the tough core. Slice the cabbage into very thin strips. Heat a large saucepan over a medium heat. When the pan is hot, add the caraway seeds and cook for a moment until they smell delicious. Add the cabbage and turn it over in the oil. Cook for a couple of minutes until the cabbage starts to soften.

Turn up the heat to high and add the wine. Allow it to bubble for a second and then season with the salt and a little pepper. Drop the heat to medium, pop a lid on the pan and cook for one hour until the cabbage is very soft. Check occasionally to make sure there is still liquid in the pan and the cabbage isn't catching. After an hour, remove the lid and cook until there is only a tiny bit of liquid left. Add the vinegar and then turn the heat down and add the butter and stir to emulsify. Keep warm while you prepare the other elements.

To make the dressing, simply mix all the ingredients together and check the seasoning. Add additional salt and pepper as needed and set aside.

If the salt beef is fridge cold, it will need steaming to heat it again. Fill a saucepan with 5 cm/2 inches of water and steam the beef in a bamboo steamer for 20–30 minutes until warmed through. If you are using the salt beef directly after cooking it, you can skip this stage.

When ready to serve, heat the oven grill/broiler to high. Put the flatbreads on a baking sheet and spread with plenty of the dressing. Cover the breads with slices of salt beef, followed by a generous amount of the quick kraut. Top with the cheese so the entire sandwich is covered. Place the stack under the grill for a couple of minutes until the cheese is melted and bubbling.

Add the Bread and Butter Pickles and a final drizzle of dressing, then cut the flatbread into quarters to serve.

Sabich – flatbread with roast aubergine, pickled egg, beetroot hummus, tahini and pickles

Sabich as a dish is a fairly modern invention. The story is that Sabich Tzvi Halabi – an Iraqi Jew who moved to Israel in the 1950s – created the sandwich in the early 1960s at a kiosk in Tel Aviv. It used the elements that are often featured in Iraqi traditional shabbat breakfasts to create a filled pita that is now widely popular in Israel but little known elsewhere.

The dish has sentimental associations for us. It was the first meal we ate when we visited Jerusalem in 2022. We ate a lot of good food on that trip, but that sabich stands out – a delicious combination of vegetables, pickles, sauces and eggs stuffed into a soft pita, eaten on plastic chairs from a hole-in-the-wall restaurant opposite the chaos of Mahaneh Yehudah Market on a Thursday night.

1 teaspoon olive oil

2 aubergines/eggplants

1 teaspoon pickle brine (preferably from the pickled tomatoes)

pinch of sumac

4 hard-boiled eggs (cooked for 6 minutes, see page 103)

HUMMUS

400-g/14-oz. can of chickpeas, drained

150 g/5$^{1}/_{2}$ oz. tahini

250 g/9 oz. Borscht-Style Pickled Beetroot (see page 46)

125 ml/$^{1}/_{2}$ cup Borscht-Style Pickled Beetroot brine (see page 46)

2 plump garlic cloves

1 tablespoon ice-cold water

$^{1}/_{2}$ teaspoon beetroot powder (optional)

TO ASSEMBLE

4 flatbreads or pitas

Instant Pickled Tomato and Cucumber Salad (see page 52)

Pink Pickled Turnips (see page 49), chopped

Pickle-Brine Tahini Dip (see page 72)

amba (tangy mango pickle condiment available from most supermarkets)

Pickled Mustard Seeds (see page 38)

best-quality olive oil, for drizzling

Makes 4 flatbreads

Heat a cast-iron frying pan/skillet over a high heat until rippingly hot. Add the oil and leave to heat slightly. Cut the aubergine into quarters lengthways, then slice each quarter into 1-cm/$^{1}/_{2}$-inch thick pieces. Add these to the hot pan and fry for about 10 minutes until cooked through and browned on all sides.

Transfer the cooked aubergine from the pan to a bowl and dress with olive oil, the pickle brine and sumac. Toss to combine and set aside for later.

Peel the hard-boiled eggs, then pickle them in pickle brine following the instructions on page 103 while you make the hummus. (If you use brine from the pickled beetroot for the eggs, they will look striking when you plate them, but any brine will work.)

To make the hummus, place the chickpeas in a food processor with a pinch of salt, the tahini, pickled beetroot, brine and garlic cloves. Blitz everything until a very smooth paste forms. Add the ice-cold water and blitz to create a creamy consistency. If you are using it, add the beetroot powder to make the hummus a vivid colour. Remove from the food processor and check the seasoning. Add more salt, if necessary.

To assemble the sabich, heat the flatbreads under the oven grill/broiler until piping hot. Spread the breads with hummus, then scatter each with pieces of dressed aubergine, followed by the pickled tomato and cucumber salad. Add the chopped pickled turnips to the pile.

Remove the hard-boiled eggs from their brine and slice each in half. Add 2 halves to each sabich, then drizzle over some amba and lots of the tahini sauce. Finish with pickled mustard seeds and a drizzle of the best olive oil.

A Bit on the Side

Pickle Bloody Mary

Nat worked in pubs for much of her twenties, which means she's spent A LOT of time mixing Bloody Marys in industrial quantities to help the people of South London get over their Saturday-night excesses. We've taken all of that experience to work up our version of this classic cocktail. It keeps all the vital ingredients – the celery salt, the horseradish, the pepper - but dials everything up a notch with the addition of a healthy whack of pickle brine.

We often make the cocktail as they do in pubs; that's to say we mix all the elements of the Bloody Mary base without the alcohol in a large bottle and keep it in the fridge. That means when you desperately need a pick-me-up, all you have to do is reach for the pre-mixed base and add booze and ice. It also means it's super easy to enjoy this as a Virgin Mary because you simply pour the pre-mix over ice and you're ready to go.

VIRGIN MARY PRE-MIX

1 litre/4 cups good-quality tomato juice

2 teaspoons tamarind paste

1 tablespoon grated fresh horseradish (in a pinch use the jarred stuff)

1 tablespoon Worcestershire sauce

juice of 1/2 lemon

1 teaspoon celery salt

1 tablespoon Shedletskys Pickleback Hot Sauce (see Note)

50 ml/3 1/2 tablespoons pickle brine (preferably the brine from Dr. Brown's Pickled Celery on page 45, Cajun Pickled Peppers on page 30 or Borscht-Style Pickled Beetroot on page 46, but you can use any pickle brine)

freshly ground black pepper

TO SERVE

ice

vodka

sherry

hot sauce of your choice

pickles, to garnish

Makes enough for 4 large Bloody Marys

Add all of the pre-mix ingredients to a jug/pitcher that will fit in the fridge. Stir well, season with plenty of black pepper and chill until you needed. The pre-mix can be made in advance and stored in the fridge for several days.

To serve, take a tall glass and half-fill with ice. Pour over 35 ml/1 1/4 fl oz. vodka and 25 ml/3/4 fl oz. sherry, then top up with about 250 ml/1 cup of the pre-mix (the exact amount will depend on the size of your glass). Adjust the flavour with additional Worcestershire sauce, pickle brine and a touch more pepper. Repeat for the remaining drinks.

Stir and garnish with a dash more hot sauce and some of the pickles that you used to make the pre-mix threaded onto a wooden skewer.

NOTES

This recipe calls for our Shedletskys Pickleback Hot Sauce because we think it really adds to the flavour, but any vinegary hot sauce would work. You could also use the Pickle Brine Hot Sauce on page 133 if you fancied making your own.

To make a Virgin Mary, follow the recipe above, but simply leave out the alcohol.

Pickle Martini

To be honest, we're not 100% sure this strictly qualifies as a true Martini. Or to be honest what even makes a Martini in the first place. The ever-reliable Savoy Cocktail Book *features four different recipes, all of which are basically just gin and vermouth in varying proportions. The more modern and no-less excellent* Meehan's Bartender Manual *says that for most of its history 'Martini' referred more to the style of glass than the booze in it.*

Whatever the origins of the cocktail, this is a delicious take that is no less lethal than its more traditional cousins. It is perhaps wetter (more vermouth) and dirtier (more brine) than purists might allow, but we urge you to give it a try before passing judgement.

We've also taken inspiration from the 'Italian' nature of the Giardiniera and opted for an Italian-style vermouth here. But this is almost purely an affectation. We think it adds a pleasant herbal note, but feel free to use any vermouth you want here. Similarly, we've made this with vodka because we think its neutral flavour allows the other elements to shine, but if you simply must have a gin Martini, knock yourself out.

40 ml/1¼ fl oz. Vaguely Italian Vegetable Giardiniera pickle brine (see page 36, for preference, but you can use any brine you have)

40 ml/1¼ fl oz. Cocchi Americano (or dry vermouth)

200 ml/6¾ fl oz. vodka

2 pieces of pickled celery from the Vaguely Italian Vegetable Giardiniera (see page 37)

4 stoned/pitted green olives

ice

Makes enough for 4 Martinis

Mix the pickle brine and vermouth in a small jug/pitcher and chill in the fridge.

At the same time, put the vodka in the freezer, along with the Martini glasses and cocktail shaker.

Leave everything to get properly frosty – at least a couple of hours – then assemble your ingredients and equipment at your bar station.

Half-fill a cocktail shaker with ice, then top with half the brine/vermouth mixture and half the vodka. Stir for a good minute until everything is extremely cold and well mixed. Alternatively, put the lid on the cocktail shaker and give it the bartender's treatment – however, this will make purists wince and your cocktails will go slightly cloudy.

Using a strainer, pour the ice-cold cocktail into two of the frozen Martini glasses. Press one of the pickled celery around the rim of the glasses and serve with an olive dropped in or added to a toothpick with a small piece of lemon peel, if liked. Repeat the process with the rest of the ingredients to make two more Martinis.

Brine spritz

There was a moment in London when suddenly Aperol spritzes were everywhere. As is the way with fads, the Aperol trend has become a cliche and trendy restaurants and bars have diversified their spritz offering to cover a huge range of bitters and flavourings. By 2024, Sam Paget Steavenson and Imme Ermgassen's wonderful Botivo seemed to emerge as the bitter of choice in all of our favourite places. We love the way this British-made aperitivo combines bittersweet backbone with herbal and citrus notes to make something that can be mixed just with soda water or used as the basis for a much more interesting spritz.

Botivo's deliciousness got us thinking whether we could use excess pickle brine as the basis for an aperitivo. After a few failed attempts (make sure you pick brines that haven't been anywhere near garlic!), we came up with this – a brine-tivo that makes a cocktail that's recognizably from the heritage of the Aperol spritz without being too burdened by its associations.

Just a note, the Brine-tivo takes about a month to infuse so make this ahead of time. If you need a faster spritz, get yourself a bottle of Botivo....

'BRINE-TIVO'

500 ml/2 cups pickle brine from sweeter pickles without any garlic (Pickled Cherries on page 62, Pickled Watermelon Rinds on page 33 or Pickled Green Tomatoes on page 61, for example)

peel of 1 orange

1 teaspoon juniper berries

1/2 teaspoon fennel seeds

sprig of fresh thyme

a thumb-sized piece of fresh ginger

100 g/3 1/2 oz. honey

250 ml/1 cup raw kombucha (either homemade or purchased – but if you are buying it, make sure the flavour complements your brine)

TO MAKE EACH SPRITZ

50 ml/1 2/3 fl oz. Brine-tivo (see above)

60 ml/2 fl oz. Prosecco (or white wine if you want to make this a Bicyclette)

30 ml/1 fl oz. soda water

pickles, to garnish

Makes a large bottle of Brine-tivo, enough for a summer's worth of cocktails

To make your own homemade brine-based aperitivo, start by straining the pickle brine into a clean container and mix with the orange peel, juniper berries, fennel seeds and thyme. Peel the ginger and slice into thin rounds and add to the container. Leave for at least one month somewhere out of direct sunlight for the flavours to infuse.

After a month, taste the brine. If you think the flavour needs more time to develop, leave it for another week. If you are happy, move on to the next stage.

Strain the brine into a large clean jug/pitcher. Add the honey and stir to dissolve. Taste again and assess whether you think the drink needs to be a little sweeter. Continue adding more honey until you are happy with the flavour.

Add the kombucha and taste again. Adjust the flavour with more honey if you think it needs it. Store in the fridge until needed (where it should last for several weeks).

To make a spritz, half-fill a glass with ice and then pour in 50 ml/1 2/3 fl oz. of the homemade Brine-tivo. Add the Prosecco or white wine before topping up with soda water. Give the spritz a stir and serve with a pickle as a garnish.

Pickle soda

There are certain things from childhood that really stick with you. For some reason, lots of food vocab taught to my year 5 French class by Mme Matin back in about 1992 remains etched in my brain.

I might never have got the opportunity to order 'une religieuse' from a patisserie – even at the time, I remember thinking that the choux buns shaped like a nun seemed overly fussy – but I have ordered my fair share of 'diabolos menthes' from village cafés across France.

The Diabolo is a uniquely French concoction – a painfully sweet and luridly coloured fruit syrup mixed with lemonade – that always seemed appealingly grown up to me. Maybe it was the way the drink was prepared that sort of looked like the barman was making a cocktail, or the fact you could usually buy cigarettes or bangers at the same time!

Thirty years after I last sang 'Moi, j'ai soif, je voudrais une diabolo menthe', we've recreated the drink using a fruity pickle brine. The result is not quite as lurid as the drinks of childhood memory, but is certainly less cloying.

SYRUP
150 g/5¹/₂ oz. Pickled Cherries (see page 62), plus extra to garnish
400 ml/1³/₄ cups brine from the pickled cherries
150 g/5¹/₂ oz. honey

TO SERVE
ice
soda water or lemonade

muslin/cheesecloth for straining

Makes about 250 ml/1 cup syrup – enough for about 8 drinks

Add the Pickled Cherries (stoned/pitted if you left them whole originally), brine and honey to a saucepan and bring to the boil over a high heat. Boil for about 30 minutes until the fruit is breaking down and the liquid has reduced by half. If the syrup becomes too thick, dilute with a little water.

Strain through a fine muslin/cheesecloth into a bottle or jar and use within one month.

To serve, add a couple of ice cubes to a tall glass and pour over 2 tablespoons of the syrup. Top with cold soda water or lemonade, garnish with a pickled or fresh cherry and enjoy.

NOTE
This technique obviously works with any pickles you have, but clearly sweeter pickles will probably result in more palatable sodas. As well as cherries, you could have a go with the pinapple salsa on page 42, the pickled celery on page 45 or even the pickled beetroot on page 46. Just keep tasting and adjust the amount of honey as needed.

Brine flights – some shots and pickle juice suggestions

Almost since the first days of Shedletskys, we've loved the idea of serving a 'Brine Flight' – a series of our pickle brines matched with shots of booze. It was something we wanted to do at our first pop-up residency before the COVID-19 pandemic put paid to that plan. So instead we kept our brine flight to ourselves, sometimes bringing out a jar of pickle juice at parties when we had some interesting booze to try.

The 'cocktail' itself is a tribute to the American tradition of chasing a shot of whiskey with a shot of pickle brine, known as a pickleback. The salty-tangy pickle brine neutralizes the booze in the same way a tequila slammer works.

As an added – and totally not supported by science – bonus, the electrolytes in pickle brine seem to help with hangovers. This means that you somehow don't feel as bad after a four-drink brine flight as you would after necking four shots of vodka.

35 ml/1¼ fl oz. booze
 (see below for suggestions)
35 ml/1¼ fl oz. appropriate pickle
 brine

TO GARNISH
a pickle from the brine
a teaspoon of dried pickle dust
 (see page 134, optional)

2 shot glasses

Makes 1 drink
(serve several combinations
to make a brine flight)

Making a pickleback is ridiculously simple; it's just a shot of booze in one glass and a shot of pickle brine in the other. You can get fancy by serving a pickle on the side, or garnishing the shot glass with pickle dust round the rim, but it really isn't critical. What is important is taking the time to think about the booze you're drinking and what pickle brine pairs nicely with it.

The classic is a shot of whiskey, Bourbon or Rye served with a shot of cucumber pickle brine, but there are lots of other options.

SOME SUGGESTIONS FOR YOUR BRINE FLIGHT

Below are just a few suggested pairings that we've had success with. Be warned, drinking shots like this makes it dangerously easy to drink a lot in short order. So go easy and pace yourself.

1   *Cajun Pickled Peppers brine (see page 30) with Cognac spiked with a dash of Peychaud's bitters*
2   *'Pukka' Pickled Watermelon Rinds brine (see page 33) with Mezcal*
3   *Vaguely Italian Vegetable Giardiniera brine (see page 37) with Grappa*
4   *Tzimmes Pickled Carrots brine (see page 41) with spiced rum*
5   *Pickled Green Tomatoes brine (see page 61) with gin*
6   *Borscht-Style Pickled Beetroot brine (see page 46) with ice-cold vodka*
7   *Pickled Cherries brine (see page 62) with Slivovitz plum brandy*
8   *Spicy Pickled Radishes brine (see page 50) with Soju*
9   *'Curtido' Southern American Pickled Cabbage brine (see page 57) with tequila*
10 *Bread and Butter Pickles brine (see page 58) with whiskey, Bourbon or Rye*

Making mustard with pickle brine

For a while, we were obsessed with trying to make mustard. We made kimchi mustard, beer mustard and pickle mustard. Whatever we attempted, we always found the results to be unpleasantly bitter, so we parked our mustard mania and moved on to other things.

Fast forward six months, we found some of our mustard experiments at the back of the cupboard and tasted them again. They were amazing, time had mellowed them out, removing the bitterness and leaving some delicious mustard that was far more interesting than anything found in a supermarket.

Even though we were happy with the results, we didn't make mustard that often. The six-month fermentation meant we really had to plan ahead if we thought we might want some mustard in the future.

While we were recipe testing for this book, we came across the technique of repeatedly rinsing mustard seeds in boiling water to remove their bitterness. It cuts the fermentation time down from six months to only one month, which means making your own mustard is much more accessible.

You can also make mustard with the pickled mustard seeds on page 38. Simply skip straight to blitzing the already pickled mustard seeds with their own brine in the ratios listed below for a double pickle mustard. Delicious.

200 g/7 oz. yellow mustard seeds
100 g/3½ oz. brown mustard seeds
boiling water, to cover
1 teaspoon salt
1 tablespoon sugar
100 ml/scant ½ cup pickle brine
50 ml/3½ tablespoons white vinegar
1 teaspoon mustard powder
2 tablespoons pickles from the same batch

Makes 1 large jar

Add the yellow and brown mustard seeds to a fine-mesh sieve/strainer. Stir with your hand to mix them evenly and place the sieve in the sink. Fill the kettle with water and boil. Pour the boiling water over the mustard seeds, making sure all of them get saturated. Repeat this with two more kettle's worth of boiling water. Once the seeds have been rinsed three times, leave them to drain, then place them in a large glass container or jar.

Boil the kettle one more time and pour 450 ml/2 cups boiling water over the mustard seeds. Cover and leave the mustard seeds to soak for 24 hours.

After 24 hours, drain the water from the mustard seeds and place them in a blender with the salt, sugar, pickle brine, vinegar and mustard powder. Blitz to a smooth paste, adjusting the consistency with a little more pickle brine if necessary. Finely chop the pickles themselves and fold through the mustard, then decant into a sterilized jar with a lid.

Store out of direct sunlight for at least one month to allow the flavours to mellow before tasting and adjusting with more salt and sugar as needed. Once you're happy with the flavour, store in the fridge for up to one year.

Pickle brine hot sauce

When all is said and done, most hot sauces (barring fermented ones like Tabasco), are essentially just vinegar, chillies/chiles and some flavourings. That means if you have a load of flavourful brine (which is just extra tasty vinegar), you have one of the critical ingredients for making your own incredible hot sauce.

The trick, as with many things, is getting the flavour pairing right. Taste the brine and think about what would go nicely with it. Find chillies that suit those flavours, add a few complementary ingredients and give it a blitz. Et voilà, your own hot sauce. Below are some rough ratios, however, the best thing to do is get tasting and see where it takes you.

300 ml/1¼ cups pickle brine

500 g/1 lb. 2 oz. appropriate and interesting chillies/chiles

100 ml/scant ½ cup appropriate vinegar

50 g/1¾ oz. pickles (from the same batch of pickle brine)

20 g/4 teaspoons salt

about 50 g/¼ cup sugar

about 2 tablespoons herbs and spices to match your brine and chillies

150–200 g/5–7 oz. fruit, vegetables, etc. (optional)

½ teaspoon xanthan gum (see Note, optional)

Makes a couple of bottles

Strain the pickle brine into a large saucepan and heat over a medium heat. De-seed the chillies (or don't, if you want a hotter hot sauce) and add them to a blender, along with the vinegar and reserved pickles. Blitz with the salt to a smooth purée. Tip this into the pickle brine and bring to a gentle simmer. Add the sugar and taste. Adjust the seasoning adding more salt and sugar as required.

At this point, decide if you want to add any additional spices or flavourings. If you decide it needs some, toast any whole spices in a dry frying pan/skillet briefly and then grind to a fine powder before adding them to the hot sauce mixture. Herbs should be simply chopped and added right at the end just before the final blitz.

Similarly when you taste the sauce, if you think it would benefit from a bit more body, consider adding some fruit or vegetables. In the past, we've added apples, pineapple, berries, cranberries, tomatoes, carrots, onion and garlic to various sauces with varying degrees of success. Remember that adding more solids will result in a thicker hot sauce so plan accordingly.

Whatever you add, remove any hard skins, stones/pits and cores and chop into rough chunks. Add to the bubbling sauce and continue to cook until the solids break down completely. Once the solids have broken down, remove the sauce from the heat and allow it to cool slightly. Tip the mixture into a blender, add ½ teaspoon xanthan gum (if using) and blitz until very smooth. Pass the sauce through a fine-mesh sieve/strainer and decant into sterilized bottles. Stored in the fridge this sauce will last for up to 6 months.

A NOTE ON XANTHAN GUM

Xanthan gum is a food additive used as a thickener, stabilizer and emulsifier. It's made from a bacteria that ferments sugar to create a sticky substance that's dried and ground into a powder. We use it to thicken and stabilize our hot sauces and stop them separating. It's easy enough to find in supermarkets in the baking section as it's used in gluten-free baking. If you're planning to make lots of hot sauce, grab some; if not, don't worry too much. Just be aware your sauce may split and need shaking before use.

Dried pickle dust

I have what I acknowledge is an annoying hatred of kitchen appliances that clutter up our kitchen counters. As a result, and much to Nat's continual irritation, we don't have a toaster or a kettle at home. We do, however, have a dehydrator. It was bought for something we wanted to cook as part of our home delivery food service, but has found regular use dehydrating excess pickles to make these flavourful dusts.

They really are a revelation. Yes, it takes a long time and yes, it's a bit messy. But the results are amazing. The drying process really intensifies the pickle flavours and it's great to be able to get a pickle hit into your food without having to always resort to adding brine or chopping up the pickles themselves. These dusts last for ages stored in airtight containers and you'll be amazed how many uses you find for them once you have them on hand.

Please note, similar results can be achieved using a regular domestic oven set to low on the fan setting, but to us seems a little wasteful to run a domestic oven continually for 36 hours. If you are going to try this in the oven, we suggest doubling, tripling or even quadrupling the quantities of pickles you dehydrate in one go. It's also worth checking whether your oven has an auto-cut off feature – pay attention to this so you don't go to bed and find the oven has turned itself off in the middle of the night!

300 g/10½ oz. pickles of your choice (try Bread and Butter Pickles on page 58, Pink Pickled Turnips on page 49 or even the Dr. Brown's Pickled Celery on page 45)

10 g/2 teaspoons salt

dehydrator or fan oven

Makes 1 small pot

Set a dehydrator to 60°C/140°F or preheat the oven to its lowest setting.

Carefully drain the pickles of all their brine while retaining any herbs and spices that were in the mix. Pat dry with paper towels, then spread them out thinly on a silicon mat.

Dry in the dehydrator or oven for at least 24 hours, or until the pickles are completely dry. For wetter pickles, this can take up to 48 hours.

When completely dry, remove the pickles from the dehydrator and immediately grind with the salt. This works best in an electric spice grinder but can also be achieved using a pestle and mortar.

Once ground to a dust, store in an airtight container for up to 3 months and use as needed to give a super pickle-y boost to chips, chicken skins or anything else that needs it.

NOTE
Over time, these dusts can clump together. It's worth pushing them through a small fine-mesh sieve/strainer with a spoon, if this happens.

Baking with brine

For a few years, I was – like lots of people – really into sourdough baking. But in recent years, I've come to the conclusion that while sourdough bread is great for toast and certain sandwiches (kimchi-cheese toasties take a bow here), in almost all other cases, it's not the best loaf for the job. Most sandwiches need something softer and less toothsome to really shine. Plus, who really has the time to properly care for their sourdough starter? However, it is true that the extra flavour you get from sourdough is a welcome upgrade to most loaves.

So, how do you get some of that sour tang into your bread without all the faff and fuss it takes to make proper naturally leavened loaves? Brine turns out to be the answer. We played around for a while with simply swapping all the water in a recipe for pickle brine with mixed results. All too often, the high acid levels stopped the yeast working properly. Instead we started using brine in a pre-starter or poolish and were very happy with the loaves it produced.

The result is this dough. The recipe uses a couple of other techniques from my sourdough days to create a versatile dough that can be as easily shaped into a loaf as it can be used for flatbreads.

POOLISH
250 g/1¾ cup strong white bread flour
250 ml/1 cup pickle brine
3 g/½ teaspoon dried yeast

DOUGH
180 ml/¾ cup lukewarm water, plus an additional 35 ml/ 2 tablespoons
6 g/1¼ teaspoons dried yeast
300 g/2 cups plus 2 tablespoons strong white bread flour
12 g/2½ teaspoons fine sea salt

Makes 1 sandwich or focaccia loaf or 6 large flatbreads

The day before you want to bake, add all the ingredients for the poolish to a large mixing bowl and mix with your hands just until they come together. Cover the bowl and leave in the fridge overnight

In the morning, remove the bowl from the fridge and take a look at the poolish. It should have increased in size a little and have a few air bubbles in it.

Add 180 ml/¾ cup lukewarm water from the tap and use your fingers to break up the poolish a little bit. Add the yeast and bread flour and mix with your hands until everything just comes together in a shaggy ball.

Alternatively, use a stand mixer fitted with the dough hook attachment for this stage. Simply put the poolish, lukewarm water, yeast and bread flour in the bowl and mix on low speed for 1 minute.

Once the dough has just started to come together, cover the bowl and leave it to sit for 25 minutes. This is known as autolysing the dough and allows the flour to absorb water and develop gluten, resulting in a more flavourful loaf.

While the dough rests, weigh out the salt in a small bowl and add the additional 35 ml/2 tablespoons lukewarm water. Stir to dissolve the salt in the water and create a brine, but don't worry if not all the salt dissolves.

After 25 minutes, add the brine to the dough, making sure all the salt is added along with the water.

Knead the dough in the bowl for 1 minute to incorporate the liquid and then tip the dough out onto a lightly floured work surface. Knead vigorously by hand for 10–12 minutes until the dough comes together into a shiny, pliable ball. You may need to add some additional flour to help prevent sticking, but do your best to add as little as possible.

Alternatively, use a stand mixer and the dough hook attachment for this stage. Mix on medium speed for 10 minutes or until the dough forms into a ball and comes away cleanly from the side of the bowl.

When the dough is pliable and smooth, lightly oil a plastic container with a lid and scoop your ball of dough into it. Turn the dough over to coat in the oil, put on the lid and leave to prove somewhere warm for 1 hour.

After an hour, using wet hands, gently slip one hand under the bottom of one side of the dough, lift and stretch it into the air, being careful not to actually break the dough. Fold this stretched dough over the top of the rest of the dough. Rotate the container 90 degrees and repeat this stretch and fold technique. Repeat the rotate, stretch and fold two more times until you have returned to your original starting position.

Replace the lid and leave the dough for another hour before repeating this stretch and fold process. Leave to rest for another hour and repeat again.

At this point, the dough should be smooth, silky and aerated with lots of bubbles. From now on, handle the dough carefully as you don't want to knock too much air out of the dough.

Tip the dough out onto a floured work surface and decide what you want to bake with it.

FOR A SANDWICH LOAF

Shape the dough into a large ball and divide into two equal pieces. Shape both pieces into neat balls and add them to a 900-g/2-pound loaf pan (about 24 x 12 x 8 cm/ 9.5 x 5 x 3 inches) with a paper liner. Leave to rise a final time for 45 minutes, or until doubled in size. Preheat the oven to 220°C/200°C fan/ 425°F/Gas 7. Bake the loaf in the preheated oven for 25 minutes. At this point, turn the oven temperature down to 180°C/160°C fan/350°F/Gas 4, lift the loaf from the tin and remove the paper liner. Return the loaf to the oven, sitting it directly on the shelf, and cook for 10 minutes on each side to develop a golden crust.

FOR A FOCACCIA LOAF (AS PICTURED)

This makes a focaccia-type loaf that works very well split horizontally for sandwiches. Lightly oil a lipped baking pan. Turn the dough out into the centre and leave it for 15 minutes to relax. Gently stretch out the dough so it fills the pan, taking care not to manhandle the dough too much. Leave it to rise for 30 minutes. Preheat the oven to 220°C/200°C/425°F/Gas 7. While the oven is heating, mix 15 ml/1 tablespoon pickle brine with 30 ml/2 tablespoons olive oil and 1 tablespoon coarse sea salt flakes in a small bowl. Using your fingers, poke holes all over the surface of the dough, then immediately pour the oil/brine mixture over the top, taking care to make sure the salt is evenly distributed across the loaf. Bake in the preheated oven for 25–30 minutes until puffed and golden.

FOR FLATBREAD

Divide the dough into 6 equal pieces and shape into balls. Using a well-floured rolling pin, roll the dough out to an even thickness of about 1 cm/½ inch. Keep the unshaped balls covered with a damp tea towel until it's time to shape and cook them. Heat a cast-iron skillet over a very high heat and when ripping hot, cook a flatbread on one side, undisturbed, for 3 minutes, then flip and cook for a further 2 minutes. Remove and keep warm wrapped in a clean dish towel or in a plastic bag while you cook the other flatbreads.

Making your own vinegar

Perhaps unsurprisingly, considering how many pickles we make, we get through a lot of vinegar. Like A LOT. We're talking hundreds of litres/gallons every week. It means that we have to opt for commercially stable and consistent distilled white vinegar so each batch of pickles comes out the same.

At home, most people don't have such constraints, which means a bit more scope to give making vinegar from scratch a go and play around with flavours.

It's really quite simple and requires only some fruit scraps, sugar and time in its most basic approach. It's also a great way of using up fruit that's past its best, as well as scraps of peel and rind that are the by-products of pickle making.

While you can make vinegar with just three ingredients, we tend to also use raw vinegar with a mother as a starter. Without it, you can still ferment everything to make vinegar but we've found things go wrong more often and you can end up with a gross-smelling jar of fruit-fly-infested water.

at least 250 g/9 oz. fruit trimmings and peel (we used the watermelon skin and flesh left over from the Pickled Watermelon Rinds, see page 33, but use whatever fruits you have to hand)

500 ml /2 cups water per 250 g/ 9 oz. fruit

$1/2$ tablespoon organic unrefined granulated cane sugar per 250 g/9 oz. fruit

1 tablespoon raw cider vinegar with mother per 250 g/9 oz. fruit

Makes 1 large bottle

First, weigh out the fruit scraps and make a note of the total weight. Place the fruit in a large glass container that's recently been cleaned and sterilized.

Use the weight you noted down to calculate how much water and sugar is needed, working to the ratio of 500 ml/2 cups water and $1/2$ tablespoon sugar per 250 g/9 oz. fruit.

Add the water to a jug/pitcher and add the right amount of sugar. Stir to dissolve. Add 1 tablespoon of raw cider vinegar per 250 g/9 oz. fruit and stir again.

Pour this mixture over the fruit scraps. Use a weight to make sure all the fruit is submerged and cover the container with a piece of muslin/cheesecloth or fine gauze. Use a rubber band to secure the fabric, then store the mix in a cupboard out of direct sunlight.

For the first 5 days, stir the mixture every morning. Leave the mixture to ferment for a total of 3–4 weeks, then strain and discard the fruit scraps.

Decant the liquid into a sterilized bottle, seal and store for another month in a dark place. After that time, taste the vinegar and use as you would any commercial vinegar. Stored in a cupboard this will last for ages: we're talking six months or beyond.

The mixture can also be used in future to make more vinegar. Just use in place of the cider vinegar in the original recipe.

Index

A

anchovies: 'mop' sauce 79
  perfect pickle potato salad 92
  pickle panzanella salad 87
apples: pickle brine apple sauce 67
  pickle slaw 95
aubergines/eggplants: sabich 116
  sesame aubergine dip 72

B

baking with brine 137–8
beef: meatball sub with pickle tomato sauce 108
  Shedletskys salt beef with boiled potatoes 83
beetroot/beet: borscht-style pickled beetroot 46
  chopped liver sandwich with pickled beetroot 112
  pickle beetroot borscht 76
  pickle beetroot tart with goat's cheese 88
  pickle loaded muffin-etta 107
  pink turnip pickles 49
Bloody Mary, pickle 121
borscht-style pickled beetroot 46
bread: chicken mayo sandwich 100
  chopped liver sandwich with pickled beetroot 112
  grilled cheese and pickle sandwich 99
  meatball sub with pickle tomato sauce 108
  pickle panzanella salad 87
  pickled egg salad sandos 103
  poolish 137–8
  Reuben flatbread with pastrami, B&B pickles, cheese and Russian dressing 115
  the Shedletskys Hot 104
  vegetarian pambazo sandwich with paprika, potatoes and hot sauce 111
bread and butter pickles 58
bread and butter raita 80
chicken mayo sandwich 100
dried pickle dust 134
perfect pickle potato salad 92

pickle cheese spread 99
pickle gravy 91
pickle-packed latkes 67
Reuben flatbread with pastrami, B&B pickles, cheese and Russian dressing 115
buttermilk: pickle-brined chicken wings with blue cheese dip 71
  ranch dressing 68

C

cabbage: curtido South American pickled cabbage 57
  'don't call it kimchi' lacto-fermented Chinese leaf cabbage 54
  pickle slaw 95
  quick kraut 115
Cajun pickled peppers 30
capers: perfect pickle potato salad 92
  pickle gravy 91
  pickle loaded muffin-etta 107
  pickle panzanella salad 87
carrots: curtido South American pickled cabbage 57
  'don't call it kimchi' lacto-fermented Chinese leaf cabbage 54
  pickle beetroot borscht 76
  pickle slaw 95
  tzimmes pickled carrots 41
  vaguely Italian vegetable giardiniera 37
cauliflower: vaguely Italian vegetable giardiniera 37
celery: Dr. Brown's pickled celery 45
  pickle slaw 95
cheese: blue cheese dip 71
  grilled cheese and pickle sandwich 99
  meatball sub with pickle tomato sauce 108
  pickle beetroot tart with goat's cheese 88
  pickle cheese spread 99
  pickle-cooked chips with pickle gravy and fried cheese 91
  pickle loaded muffin-etta 107

Reuben flatbread with pastrami, B&B pickles, cheese and Russian dressing 115
cherries: pickle soda 126
  pickled cherries 62
chicken: chicken mayo sandwich 100
  pickle brine chicken curry 80
  pickle-brined chicken wings with blue cheese dip 71
  the Shedletskys Hot 104
chicken livers: chopped liver sandwich with pickled beetroot 112
chicken skin with pickle dust 75
chickpeas: hummus 116
chillies/chiles: lacto-pickled pineapple salsa 42
  pickle brine chicken curry 80
  pickle brine hot sauce 133
  vaguely Italian vegetable giardiniera 37
Chinese leaf cabbage, 'don't call it kimchi' lacto-fermented 54
chips, pickle-cooked 91
Cocchi Americano: pickle Martini 122
cold brining 14, 18
cucumber: bread and butter pickles 58
  bread and butter raita 80
  classic deli dill-pickled cucumber 29
  instant pickled tomato and cucumber salad 53
  pickle panzanella salad 87
curry, pickle brine chicken 80
curtido: curtido South American pickled cabbage 57
  pickle slaw 95

D

daikon: 'don't call it kimchi' lacto-fermented Chinese leaf cabbage 54
deep-fried pickles with ranch dressing 68
dill-pickled cucumber 29
dips: blue cheese dip 71
  pickle tahini dip 72
  ranch dressing 68
  sesame aubergine dip 72
Dr. Brown's pickled celery 45

'don't call it kimchi' lacto-fermented Chinese leaf cabbage 54
dressings: ranch dressing 68
  Reuben dressing 115
drinks: brine flights 129
  brine spritz 125
  pickle Bloody Mary 121
  pickle Martini 122
  pickle soda 126

E

eggs: chopped liver sandwich with pickled beetroot 112
  pickled egg salad sandos 103
  sabich 116
English muffins: pickle loaded muffin-etta 107

F

fennel: vaguely Italian vegetable giardiniera 37
fermented pickles 20–3
fish: 'mop' sauce 79
  perfect pickle potato salad 92
  pickle panzanella salad 87
  flatbreads 137–8
  Reuben flatbread with pastrami, B&B pickles, cheese and Russian dressing 115
  sabich 116
flavour, adding 13
focaccia 137–8
fruit trimmings and peel: homemade vinegar 141

G

gherkins: deep-fried pickles 68
giardiniera: meatball sub with pickle tomato sauce 108
  pickle loaded muffin-etta 107
  pickle panzanella salad 87
  pickle tomato sauce 108
  vaguely Italian vegetable giardiniera 37
giardiniera pickle brine: pickle Martini 122
gochugaru chilli/chile flakes: 'don't call it kimchi' lacto-fermented Chinese leaf cabbage 54
  spicy pickled radishes 50
gravy, pickle 91

H

honey: pickle soda 126
  tzimmes pickled carrots 41
horseradish: pickle Bloody
  Mary 121
  Reuben dressing 115
hot brining 14, 19
hot sauce: pickle brine hot
  sauce 133
  the Shedletskys Hot 104
  vegetarian pambazo
    sandwich with paprika,
    potatoes and hot sauce
    111
hummus 116

J K

jalapeño chillies/chiles:
  lacto-pickled pineapple
  salsa 42
Kentucky roast lamb with
  black brine 'mop' sauce 79
kombucha: brine spritz 125
kraut, quick 115

L

labne, plain 72
lacto-fermented pickles:
  'don't call it kimchi'
    lacto-fermented Chinese
    leaf cabbage 54
  lacto-pickled pineapple
    salsa 42
lamb: Kentucky roast lamb
  with black brine 'mop' sauce
  79
latkes, pickle-packed 67

M

Martini, pickle 122
matzo meal: pickle-packed
  latkes 67
  the Shedletskys Hot 104
mayonnaise: blue cheese dip
  71
  chicken mayo sandwich 100
  pickled egg salad sandos
    103
  ranch dressing 68
  Reuben dressing 115
meatball sub with pickle
  tomato sauce 108
mescal: 'pukka' pickled
  watermelon rinds 33
'mop' sauce 79
muffin-etta, pickle loaded 107
mustard seeds: mustard with
  pickle brine 130
  pickled mustard seeds 38

O P

olives: pickle loaded
  muffin-etta 107
  vaguely Italian vegetable
    giardiniera 37
onions, sweet/sour sumac
  pickled 34
pambazo sandwich,
  vegetarian 111
panzanella salad, pickle 87
party platter, pickle 72
pastrami: Reuben flatbread
  with pastrami, B&B pickles,
  cheese and Russian
  dressing 115
pears: 'don't call it kimchi'
  lacto-fermented Chinese
  leaf cabbage 54
peppers: Cajun pickled
  peppers 30
  pickle slaw 95
  vaguely Italian vegetable
    giardiniera 37
Persian cucumber: classic deli
  dill-pickled cucumber 29
pickle brine: brine flights 129
  brine spritz 125
  brine-tivo 125
  'mop' sauce 79
  mustard with pickle brine
    130
  pickle beetroot borscht 76
  pickle Bloody Mary 121
  pickle brine chicken curry
    80
  pickle brine hot sauce 133
  pickle-brined chicken wings
    with blue cheese dip 71
  pickle soda 126
  pickle tahini dip 72
  poolish 137–8
  Shedletskys salt beef with
    boiled potatoes 83
  vegetarian pambazo
    sandwich with paprika,
    potatoes and hot sauce 111
pickle dust, dried 134
  chicken skin with pickle
    dust 75
pineapple: lacto-pickled
  pineapple salsa 42
pink turnip pickles 49
poolish 137–8
potatoes: perfect pickle
  potato salad 92
  pickle-cooked chips 91
  pickle-packed latkes 67
  Shedletskys salt beef with
    boiled potatoes 83

vegetarian pambazo
  sandwich with paprika,
  potatoes and hot sauce
  111
Prosecco: brine spritz 125
'pukka' pickled watermelon
  rinds 33

R

radishes: chicken mayo
  sandwich 100
  pickle slaw 95
  spicy pickled radishes 50
raisins: tzimmes pickled
  carrots 41
raita, bread and butter 80
ranch dressing 68
ratios 17
Reuben dressing 115
Reuben flatbread with
  pastrami, B&B pickles,
  cheese and Russian
  dressing 115
ricotta: pickle beetroot tart 88

S

sabich 116
salads: instant pickled tomato
  and cucumber salad 53
  perfect pickle potato salad
    92
  pickle panzanella salad 87
  pickle slaw 95
salami: pickle loaded
  muffin-etta 107
salsa, lacto-pickled pineapple
  42
salt beef: Reuben flatbread
  with pastrami, B&B pickles,
  cheese and Russian
  dressing 115
  Shedletskys salt beef with
    boiled potatoes 83
sandwiches 96–117
sauces: pickle brine apple
  sauce 67
  pickle brine hot sauce 133
  pickle tomato sauce 108
sesame aubergine dip 72
shawarma, pickled vegetable
  84
the Shedletskys Hot 104
Shedletskys' quick pickle
  method 10–13
Shedletskys salt beef with
  boiled potatoes 83
slaw, pickle 95
soda water: brine spritz 125
  pickle soda 126

spicy pickled radishes 50
spread, pickle cheese 99
sterilization 19
storing pickles 13, 18
sweet/sour sumac pickled
  onions 34

T

tahini: hummus 116
  pickle tahini dip 72
tamarind paste: pickle Bloody
  Mary 121
tart: pickle beetroot tart with
  goat's cheese 88
tequila: 'pukka' pickled
  watermelon rinds 33
tomato juice: pickle Bloody
  Mary 121
tomatoes: green tomatoes 61
  instant pickled tomato and
    cucumber salad 53
  pickle brine chicken curry
    80
  pickle loaded muffin-etta
    107
  pickle panzanella salad 87
  pickle tomato sauce 108
Turkish peppers: Cajun
  pickled peppers 30
turmeric: bread and butter
  pickles 58
turnip pickles, pink 49
tzimmes pickled carrots 41

V

vegetables: pickle party
  platter with dips 72
  pickled vegetable
    shawarma 84
  preparation tips 13
  vaguely Italian vegetable
    giardiniera 37
vegetarian pambazo
  sandwich with paprika,
  potatoes and hot sauce
  111
vermouth: pickle Martini 122
vinegar 17, 141
  vinegar brined pickles
    14–19
vodka: pickle Martini 122

W Y

watermelon rind, 'pukka'
  pickled 33
yogurt: bread and butter raita
  80
  pickle slaw 95
  plain labne 72

Acknowledgements

Nat and I would love to extend our warmest thanks to everyone who has helped along the Shedletskys journey.

Our parents Marion and Paul Cooper and David and Linda Preston, for their endless support and assistance at the Pickle Palace. Nick Preston for uncomplainingly filling and labelling thousands of jars week in, week out. The rest of our families – Will, Cara, Astrid and Zephyr – for lots of wise words and useful suggestions.

And, of course, Freda Cooper, née Shedletsky, for inspiring the whole venture in the first place.

The whole team at Ryland Peters & Small, and especially Editorial Director Julia Charles, for asking us to create the book and their immeasurable help putting it together. Plus, photographer Mowie Kay, food stylist Troy Willis and the rest of the shoot team for making our food look incredible.

Finer Things Club members Emily, Charlotte, Matt, Sean and Dan for all the dinners, chats and laughs along the way that helped inspire many of the recipes and resulted in the earliest drafts of the book. Plus Claire and Henry for standing with us at our first ever market stall and keeping us company – without you Shedletksys might have ended before it even began.

Each and every one of the brilliant cookbook authors in our collection who've been a continual source of inspiration.

Our wonderful stockists around the country, and finally, every single lovely Shedletskys customer who's purchased a jar of pickles or a bottle of hot sauce. The Make Away gang that kept us going through lockdown and whose feedback and comments helped refine our cooking style.

We love you all. Feeding you has been our pleasure.